STATE- SPONSORED SEX

AND OTHER TALES OF INTERNATIONAL MISADVENTURE

CLAIRE NOBLE

Claire Noble

Shanghai, Hong Kong, Zurich, Las Vegas, Vail

Copyright © 2014 by Claire Noble.

All rights reserved. No part of this publication may be reproduced, distributed or transmitted in any form or by any means, including photocopying, recording, or other electronic or mechanical methods, without the prior written permission of the publisher, except in the case of brief quotations embodied in critical reviews and certain other noncommercial uses permitted by copyright law. For permission requests, write to the publisher, addressed "Attention: Permissions Coordinator," at the address below.

Claire Noble
P.O. Box 4039
Edwards, CO 81632
www.clairenoble.org

Please Note: This is a work of creative non-fiction. All events were depicted essentially as the author remembered them, with some creative license. In some instances names and details were changed.

Book Layout ©2013 BookDesignTemplates.com

State-Sponsored Sex and other Tales of International Misadventure/ Claire Noble. -- 1st ed.
ISBN-13: 978-1494703158

Contents

BC: Before China 1
1999 7
Axe-Murdering Troll Seeks Same 13
Dating by the Rules 23
The Other Side of the Compass 33
Cultural Diversions 41
Stepford Villas 49
State-Sponsored Sex 55
Chinese Fire Drill 61
I Say Doufu, You Say Tofu 69
Really Desperate Housewife 75
Rub Me the Wrong Way 81
Beauty Schooled 87
Shocked Up 93
Birth in the Time of Plague 99
Foreign Objects 103
Tough Titties 113
Market Driven 119
Stretch Goal 129
Up the Yin Yang 135
The Kim and I 141
Not What I Expected 147
Sweet Nothings 155
Waste Management 159
Religiously Incorrect 165
Smuggler's Poos 169
Up To and Including Voodoo 173

Dickens Lives 183
Oh No He Didn't 189
The Distance Between Heaven and Here 195
Rocky Mountain Redeye 201
The Bitch in the Kitchen 209
Riley's Wife 215
Dancing with Erica Jong 221

For Mark

*A good laugh and a long sleep
are the two best cures for anything.*

–Irish Proverb

ONE

BC: BEFORE CHINA

My relocation to China was relatively abrupt and impulsive. In truth, that aptly characterized most of my life planning, but I was on the wrong side of thirty for that to continue to be acceptable, yet I could not resist when once again, adventure called. Growing up in the pre-cable era in a desiccated West Texas town, excitement consisted of Miller Lite-induced intoxication at desert bonfires and the arrival of non-network television. It did not seem obvious at the time, but the excitement of underage drinking and MTV had a limited shelf life. I may have craved adventure, but I had no idea what to expect. Much like 1950s predictions of life in the twenty-first century, my concept of life beyond the El Paso city limits was not entirely fact based.

For instance, my initial insights into the venerable and ancient culture of the Orient came courtesy of the Peking Palace restaurant in El Paso, Texas. It was there waiting tables that I learned the intricacies of Chinese cuisine, like how to properly fold a mu shu pork pancake. Furthermore, I learned that the Chinese serve steamed rice with every meal and conclude their meals with fortune cookies. My education went beyond the culinary to encompass the cultural too. I learned that those born in the year of the snake like myself were wise and wealthy, but also vain and selfish. A middle-class teenager at the time, I would have gladly accepted the latter, provided the former also came true. I should have mated with an ox or a rooster, but wound up with a rabbit instead. The ox symbolizes wealth and the rooster good fortune, but at least the rabbit was a sign of good luck in both East and West, parts of it anyway. Life planning courtesy of a paper placemat in a Chinese restaurant likely called into question the wisdom I allegedly possessed.

    Tired of cleaning up the remains of discarded fortune cookies robbed of their predictions and left broken and uneaten on the table, I, the wise snake, began telling customers that if they wanted their fortunes to come true, they had to eat the cookie. Uneaten cookies, I advised, go rogue, and not only do their fortunes not come true, the opposite may occur. I proudly dispensed what I thought at the time sounded like ancient Chinese wisdom. I would later learn that my Chinese cultural education had been a sham. The mu shu pork served in America bears only a passing resemblance to its ancestor on the mainland, nearly half of the Chinese do not even eat rice, and fortune cookies are apparently one of the few things not invented in China. Worse still, the proprietor of the Peking Palace was not really Chinese; Larry was from Taiwan.

For years, I also thought Chinese food was my favorite cuisine. That was before I set foot in China and had *Chinese* Chinese food. Eating out in China, I was initially dismayed by the absence of Sterno-equipped pupu platters, tropical-drink umbrellas and moo goo gai pan. Even when menus came with photos, I often did not recognize what I was looking at, despite the fact that the dishes often contained eyes that were staring back at me. What I found most distressing was that fortune cookies were replaced with orange slices. I felt robbed of my rightful post-meal prophecy. My indignation was misplaced. Oranges are a symbol of luck in China, and they are offered after the meal as a wish for good fortune and a sweet life. Although the element of risk was lost with the elimination of fortune cookies, the vitamin C content of the meal was vastly improved. Over time, I would find food I liked, loved even. But one conviction never changed; red bean paste is not an acceptable dessert ingredient.

Furthermore, there was no point hissing to my dinner guests that I was born in the year of the snake when there were no placemats on the table depicting the Chinese zodiac and the clearly superior snake attributes. I was not even certain the Chinese zodiac applied to non-Chinese, but I preferred my Chinese sign to my Western one—Libra. I liked being a predator rather than an inanimate object. Being a snake does have its drawbacks, like swallowing a meal whole and then lying around with an enormous bulge waiting for it to digest. Fortunately this only happens to me when I overindulge in Mexican food.

After having spent my first eighteen years in the asshole end of Texas, I was ready to go—anywhere. Blame it on the parched suburbia I grew up in. The wide expanses of asphalt and concrete of my youth were cruelly named for Edenic, tropical locations. I grew up on Trinidad Drive, which paralleled Honolulu. My best friend lived on Monaco. Our neighborhood street names were chosen from fantasy locations throughout the world. The adjacent neighborhood was named for locations throughout Ireland. The common theme seemed to be places that were green and supported vegetation, something my town did not.

El Paso was not only brown, it was downright dangerous. My parents chose to remain in Texas when my father retired from the military after his tour in Vietnam. Low property prices rather than family ties persuaded two New Yorkers to settle in West Texas, which explains my inability to say "y'all" and lack of acquaintance with any of my extended family. My parents made their decision when El Paso was still a benign, smallish town. Unfortunately, it was the conjoined twin of what became known as one of the most dangerous cities in the northern hemisphere, Juarez, Mexico. Drug wars were not the only reason for El Paso's malignancy; the sun was the other. My siblings

State-Sponsored Sex

and I were forced to grow up where no person of Irish descent was designed to inhabit in the pre-SPF era. The town I grew up in was trying to kill me.

I escaped El Paso, destined for college, early on an August morning in the year made infamous by George Orwell, 1984. I said good-bye to my father through his closed bedroom door.

He bellowed back at me, "Remember, you're there to learn, not have a good time."

Advice I never forgot, and never heeded. Even as my mother stood waving in her white nightgown from the sidewalk, tears streaming down her face at the departure of her youngest child, I wore an exuberant smile. I drove away from my parents' ranch-style home with its rock-landscaped front yard, heading east for Austin in my Volkswagen Rabbit with its leaky sunroof. I did not know where life was leading me, but as long as it was away from El Paso, I was ready to go.

Four years later, I graduated with a Liberal Arts degree from the University of Texas, prompting my father to predict my imminent starvation due to my unemployable degree. A fan of eating, I joined the air force. If all went according to plan, I would embark on four years of fun and adventure, maybe even visit some of the exotic destinations whose names had graced the street signs of my hometown. And I would get paid. During that time, I would figure out what I really wanted to do with the rest of my life. It seemed like a brilliant plan at the time. The first place the air force sent me was to Albuquerque, New Mexico, a four-hour drive north of El Paso and more desert. The second place they sent me, Saudi effing Arabia. The karmic implications were undeniable. Trinidad, Honolulu and Monaco would have to wait.

Because I possessed only a vague notion of what I wanted my life to be, I was happy to abdicate the hard decision making to my employer, the U.S. government. Yes, I trusted a massive bureaucratic machine to make life-changing decisions for me. For the duration of my brief military career I was not the master of my fate, I was its bitch. Thanks to the United States Air Force, in the span of seven years I moved seven times and held as many jobs. By my thirties I was growing weary of the nomadic life. I did eventually get to live in some exotic and green locations, such as Korea and Japan. However, rather than pursuing a life of fun and adventure, I began to desire stability and belonging. I decided to pull the plug on the machine and run my own life. I thought I was ready to put adventure behind me. It was as though I had never met me.

TWO

....

1999

As 1999 approached, China was still a foreign concept to me. I remained unaware it would soon figure far more prominently in my life. My road to China passed through Virginia. More than a decade had elapsed since I waited tables at the Peking Palace, and my knowledge of China had expanded slightly with the help of Gong Li movies: primarily images of red lanterns, sounds of Chinese opera and the feeling of dismay that Chinese movies were incapable of any ending other than tragic.

Parting ways with the United States Air Force, I attended job fairs specifically intended to recruit young military officers exiting the service. I was offered numerous positions throughout the country: marketing in San Antonio, recruitment in Austin and sales in Atlanta. I chose consulting in northern Virginia. My decision was not made for purely professional reasons. In fact, it was chosen only for romantic reasons. The job was an afterthought; my limited vision could not see beyond a guy. I met Henry Hanford years before, but he was married at the time. Shortly before my separation from the air force was official, Henry sent me an email.

"My wife has left me. Maybe there is a chance for us now?"

Henry held a high-level government position in the D.C. area. He told me it was my decision, but that if we were to have a chance, I needed to live near him. I chose Henry, and three months after I moved to Virginia to be near him, his wife returned, and he chose her. My life was a Chinese movie.

As much as I wanted to pack all my stuff in my car and go home, there was no home to go to. My parents had divorced a few years earlier. Subsequently, both had found new partners and relocated to other arid locales; my mom moved to Las Vegas and my dad to Dallas. I wish I could say I stayed in Virginia because it was the adult thing to do, but I did not do it out of maturation. I stayed in Virginia out of false hope that Henry would change his mind. He never did.

Armed with a more practical graduate degree in management, a military contractor hired me to provide business-process-improvement consulting to a Navy procurement office. The manager who hired me promised interesting work where I would learn new things every day. I suspect he was a former military recruiter who promised enlistees five-star accommodations, gourmet meals and unlimited access to guns and ammo. The only new things I learned daily were the lunch specials at the Lebanese deli by my office.

Consultant was not something I ever claimed I wanted to be when I grew up, and now I knew why. It was not hard work, but it managed to be dismal work in an astonishing number of ways. The office where I worked was a converted windowless storage space located deep within the bowels of a government office building. I am no expert, but I suspect that work cave was a feng shui disaster. The bad karma of our office location was offset, however, by the hygiene relief our bathrooms provided to the local homeless population.

Chronically cancelled meetings and a near perfect record of unreturned phone calls were prominent clues that the navy office I was assigned to was less interested in working with me than I was with them. Once I realized that their work was as boring as it sounded, I was more relieved than offended. The problem was, I had to produce something in order to get paid. My firm billed the government $500,000 annually for my services, of which I was paid the inequitable portion of $40,000. I think drug mules got a better cut. Still, I had to have something to show for that forty grand. I doubted my employer was unique among military contractors that charge massive amounts for dubious services from the bloated defense budget, hoping no one will notice. Ninety-nine percent of the time, they were right.

When my colleague, Pak Kyoh, left our firm to work for the D.C. government, he said he would keep me in mind if anything opened up. A few months later he emailed me about a newly created position as an employee trainer in the mission-support office. Eager to escape my life as a character in a *Dilbert* comic strip, I reread *What Color is Your Parachute?* and prepared responses to a wide range of potential questions, all with appropriate anecdotes. I spent evenings and weekends creating a PowerPoint presentation showcasing my plan for creating a management-training program tailored to the district's needs. I made copies of the presentation at Kinko's to provide as handouts. I attended three separate interviews and sounded like the expert I was not. However, I also ignored one of the basic tenets of the unlucky: things could always get worse.

Perhaps I should have anticipated impending doom when the department director skeptically asked me, "Are you sure you want to work *here?*" before formally offering me the position.

I got the training job and an express journey to perdition. Hell was not a place in the afterlife. Hell was a human resources office within the government of the District of Columbia during the waning days of the Marion Berry administration—the infamous mayor on crack.

I created my program and built a team of trainers. Together we delivered training to middle managers throughout the city government. The classes provided by my team of trainers were met with appreciation and praise wherever they were offered. At the same time, I

State-Sponsored Sex

earned the loathing and enmity of my coworkers in HR. Familiarity may breed contempt, but so does success. After a year of enduring active sabotage, like having my computer purloined and subtle snubs like people exiting elevators rather than ride with me, I'd had enough.

Monster.com intervened like an early release program. I traded bureaucracy for bucolic and left the D.C. government, with its seventy-five-hour workweeks, and moved to the Virginia countryside. Huthwaite, Inc., arguably the country's premier sales training company, hired me. Huthwaite's headquarters were at Wheatland Manor near Leesburg, VA. Cows grazed in pastures on one side of the property while vineyards ran in gnarled stripes along the other. My job was to interview our clients' top salespeople about their products, industry and competitors. That information was then used to create sales training specific to their sales force. Not only was the work fascinating, but Huthwaite was also a laboratory for innovative motivational workforce techniques. Kindness and civility would have been enough, but in addition to friendly coworkers, there were mini-muffins, interoffice bonuses and two shaggy Irish wolfhounds. It was as if I had been released from hell on a technicality. My belief in miracles, dormant since elementary school, was renewed.

In my own personal version of a harmonic convergence, the future in general and mine in particular were aligned and improving. Even though I resembled Wilma Flintstone, I felt like Jane Jetson. I could not live without my Sonicare, cell phone and Internet access, none of which had even existed only a few years prior, and at least two of which were probably made in China. The ominous forecasts of the Y2K digital implosion, with predictions of mass computing system failures due to the practice of designating years only by the last two digits, did not diminish the turn-of-the-century excitement but gave the moment a frisson of peril. We had the technology, but on January 1, 2000, the question that loomed over the dawn of a new century was whether or not coffee makers would work in the morning. It was not that I did not care, growing up while Reagan was president, I had always been fascinated with the prospect of a post-apocalyptic world. However, at that moment all that mattered was that I finally got to party like it was 1999. Unfortunately, I still had no one to party with, but at least I was finally interviewing candidates.

THREE

AXE-MURDERING TROLL SEEKS SAME

Getting dumped by Henry mere months after moving across the country for him was a low point in my life, but it had plenty of company. Most episodes in my hall of shame involved drinking without restraint or speaking without thinking. Drunk-dialing exes and staff-meeting malapropisms mortified me still, years later. However, most of my unfortunate behavior was confined to my college years and early twenties. I would not be the first person to say a silent prayer of thanks that mobile phones equipped with cameras did not exist during my misspent youth. My decision to join Henry, however, was made in the sober light of day a decade later. Furthermore, in the past I distanced myself from my embarrassing behavior as quickly as possible. Unfortunately, after Henry, I was trapped in a seemingly inescapable vortex of dating indignities.

My manicurist arranged my first and last blind date, ever. He was more than thirty years older than me and drove a red Trans Am, not vintage. When he took me to dinner he asked for a senior discount on his meal, and the waitress asked if I wanted my meal discounted also. When I pointed out the age disparity to my manicurist at my next appointment, she protested that I had claimed to prefer older men.

"By older I meant three to five years, not three to five decades."

I did not find out until the first meeting that the Smithsonian Singles program I enrolled in was the place to meet for singles over fifty. Thanks to these incidents, my friends began teasing me that I checked a potential date's AARP status before agreeing to go out with them. Other avenues for meeting men had also failed me: my co-workers and my tennis class were exclusively female and my church was gay-friendly—lots of terrific guys whose only communication with me consisted of criticism for reading the Responsorial Psalm too fast. If the Internet could find me a cool job, maybe it could also find me a guy, preferably one no longer encumbered by student loans but not yet eligible for 401K withdrawals, that sweet spot where erections did not require pharmaceutically enabled augmentation.

1999 was the primordial era of Internet dating, with the number of Internet users still a small, selective demographic—predominantly college-educated and male. For a female wading into the online dating world at that time, it truly was raining men. Rather than the hordes trolling online dating sites today, then the trolls

State-Sponsored Sex

were easily distinguishable from suitable candidates for matrimony. Come on, I was thirty-four years old, one more year until I reached the ominous age when urban legend had it I stood a better chance of experiencing a terrorist attack than the sacrament of marriage. In 1999, Osama Bin Laden had yet to become a household name.

For days, I agonized over the details of my personal ad. It seemed prudent to be truthful if I ever actually wanted to meet any potential suitor in person. Blue-eyed was the only trait I possessed that most men seemed to be looking for—the other two being tall and blonde. Therefore, I decided to play to my strengths and try the witty approach:

"Axe-murdering troll seeks same. Just kidding. I'm short with freckles and red hair. I am impressed with my driving skills—my passengers less so. I work out to support my food habit. I play tennis and ski—both badly. I love to travel, read and watch movies. I live in a townhouse, not under a bridge. I own a hammer and a wrench—but no axe."

I also realized that my criteria for selecting datable men were no longer adequate. Sadly, beyond cute and witty, I had no criteria. In a metro area where women outnumbered men, the cruel capitalism of supply and demand dictated the rules of dating. I was consigned to scraping up leftovers from the floor. As a result of this open-door policy, I dated a Korean immigrant whose mother wanted me dead, a chef with a slight substance-abuse problem and a ballroom-dancing enthusiast.

Actually, in addition to his agility and grace on the dance floor, the ballroom dancer was highly educated and multilingual. He read Alexandre Dumas in French. But he was also young, noncommittal and Jewish. I did not have a bias against Jews, but after my experience with the Korean mother, I was not interested in finding out if the Jewish mother had a bias against me. I may not have had criteria, but mothers do. One already decided that I was imperiling her family's genetic legacy, "Those blue eyes, so ugly." Surely imperiling another's spiritual legacy would be just as contentious. Shakespeare was right: dating someone under a cloud of family disapproval can lead to sword fights, poison and tragic consequences.

Actually, the primary reason I did not pursue a relationship with the dancer was for a more secular reason, I cannot dance. I have to concentrate to clap in time to music. Unless it was the Macarena, dancing required a partner of the opposite sex to dance with. I could never be his partner, and it would have been torture to watch him glide across dance floors, arms entwined with graceful and poised women while I glowered from my seat in the non-rhythm section. We were doomed.

To put an end to these serial mismatches, I needed to determine exactly what I was looking for. The first draft of my list of requirements contained forty-three attributes. Upon careful consideration, I decided to ease my transition from insufficient standards to excessive standards and whittled the list down to thirteen desirable traits: optimistic, intelligent, educated, funny, sophisticated, well-traveled, physically fit, well-dressed, successful, handsome, thirty-five to forty-five years old, dog lover and a gentleman. All the traits my meager dating pool had lacked.

Axe-murderers and trolls—that was what I told myself would be in my net when I logged onto my computer the next morning. Thankfully, there was not one guy on the FBI's Most Wanted List or from a Grimm's fairy tale. Instead, I received scores of inquiries from men throughout the country. I went out with five guys who lived in my area. One was a new chiropractor in turmoil about his choice of profession. Two others, not surprisingly, were software developers. Roger Grubbs was a successful business owner. He was cute, so we went out several times. Bad habits are the hardest ones to break.

After visiting a farmers' market and antiquing one Saturday afternoon, he surprised me with an impromptu dinner invitation with close friends who had just returned from living overseas. We went back to his apartment so he could change. We did not have time to go by my apartment so I could change. I protested that I could not go to dinner because "I looked like a grub." An uncomfortable silence ensued. I apologized, and he laughed it off. The relationship never recovered. To be honest, I did not want a last name that was another word for larva. Besides, he kissed like a Chihuahua on meth.

Truth was, I was feeling picky again. It was as if the universal balance had been restored. I continued a correspondence with a fellow in Northern New Jersey. Mr. New Jersey regaled me with anecdotes about his exciting life including single-malt tours of Scotland, box seats at the US Open and dinners at trendy Manhattan restaurants. His photo was posted online along with his profile. He was handsome, but the chemistry was lost in the dial-up connection. Although I was neutral about his photo, his emails were so interesting and witty I kept up the correspondence. I had yet to make the technological leap to digital, so my profile had no photo. He requested I send him one, probably trying to determine just how short and how freckly I really was. I sent him the most recent photo I could find from a wedding I had attended a year earlier, and cut off the half with my Korean ex-boyfriend in it. He suggested we meet the next time he was in Washington.

Two months after our initial email exchange, I met the fifth bachelor from my Internet dating experiment. I was a few minutes late, which was, in fact, early for me. At 6:07 on a cool October evening, I stepped into The Old Ebbitt Grill, across the street from the White House, and turned to face the bar. Mark was wearing a sports coat, no tie. He turned to face me with a wide smile of even, straight teeth. He looked better than I expected. I tried not to gasp.

"Punctuality isn't one of my strengths. I hope it isn't on your list of requirements," I explained as I approached the bar. Under pressure, I have the tendency to say the stupidest thing that comes to mind.

"I don't have a list. Do you have a list?" he said while standing to greet me. He was just taller than average, with hair showing the first signs of distinction.

"Have you ordered something to drink? Boy, I could sure use a gin and tonic." I gave him my best job-interview handshake and tried to act casual. I feared, however, that my face looked more maniacal than casual—rigidly fixed in a goofy grin. Fortunately the bartender quickly delivered my gin and tonic. I took a few gulps. Consuming liquid prevented me from saying anything else that might sabotage the evening.

We finished our drinks and set out for dinner. Outside the bar, we slipped into a taxi idling at curbside.

"Kinkead's," I told the driver. Kinkead's was considered one of D.C.'s top restaurants.

"Great choice," Mark said after the hostess had seated us at a table with a view of the entire restaurant.

"What looks good?" he asked me after we had studied the menu a few minutes, which was a welcome respite from the burden of witty banter.

"I was thinking of the salmon. It comes with *haricot verts*, I wonder what those are?" I pronounced every consonant as if it were an English phrase.

"That's ah-ree-koh vehr," Mark said, supplying the proper French pronunciation. "It means green beans," he added, laughing.

"Then why didn't they just write 'green beans'?" I muttered, wondering when green beans became so pretentious.

Later during the meal, he asked, "How do you define petite?"

"Well, the standard criterion is 5'4" and under. At 5'3" and a smidgen, I meet the criteria."

"Oh, so petite is only height? A woman can be short and big and still be considered petite."

"Right. Why do you ask?" I said as I slowly set down my fork and wondered what he was insinuating.

"I was, uh, surprised by the size of some of my previous dates. Women tend to shave a few pounds off their estimates."

"Oh," I said, relieved. "Well, I did some opposition research before writing my ad."

"Oh?" Mark said and raised one eyebrow, very Spock-like.

"Sure, I came across an article in *Maxim* magazine that compared male versus female vocabulary used in personal ads. For instance, according to *Maxim*, when a woman writes 'petite' she is probably 'freakishly short' and when she writes 'voluptuous,' think 'fat.' I tried to be specific to avoid any misunderstanding. Maybe I just got lucky, but I found most guys to be truthful, except the guy who failed to mention he had suffered a stroke and was partially paralyzed."

"Whoa. How old was he?"

State-Sponsored Sex

"Not old," I protested. "We met at an Applebee's. When I commented on the jackass who had parked his convertible red Porsche in the handicapped parking spot, he told me it was his car. Congenital heart defect. He'd regained movement in his leg so he could walk, but he still received physical therapy to improve movement in his left arm. Still, though, a nice guy."

"Well, you're a *coup de foudre*."

"What's that French for, cauliflower?"

"No," he said, laughing again. "Something wonderful."

"Oh, thank you." I thought it literally meant "something wonderful." I had no idea at the time it meant love at first sight. If I had known that, it would have saved me a lot of angst, or scared the hell out of me. Either way, I felt as if I was finally emerging from the pathetic morass I had been in since my unceremonious dumping by Henry.

FOUR

DATING BY THE RULES

Mark and I did not talk until dawn. In fact, the conversation plodded along for a little more than two hours, the time it took to eat our three-course meal. After drinks and dinner, our evening ended with a chaste hug in front of the parking garage where I had parked my emerald green Volvo 850. I was indecisive enough to be aloof. Besides, I had read *The Rules* and was taking an old-school approach to dating. I was not looking for hookups because I was on a mission. The cashier at Barnes and Noble had rolled his eyes at me a few weeks earlier when he saw *The Rules* in my stack of purchases. The book unabashedly promised to deliver a foolproof strategy for snagging a husband. What did I have to lose?

"You know this is bullshit, right?" he asked, losing his battle with self-control.

"My current approach isn't working," I said. "I need professional help."

"Well, this isn't going to get you a husband," he said.

We'll see about that, I thought.

I offered to show Mark a local's favorite for Saturday morning breakfast, the Eastern Market in the Capitol Hill neighborhood. First date and I was already breaking a rule. I was taking a calculated risk asking him out so early in our relationship, if it could be called that yet, and was relieved when he enthusiastically agreed. Over dinner, he admitted he had just had a birthday. This definitely placed him outside my preferred age range and fourteen years older than me. I had not made up my mind as to whether or not this trait was negotiable. I decided to wait and see how he did on the twelve remaining characteristics.

After arranging to meet the following morning, I raced to the nearest Total Wine before it closed to pick him up a bottle of my favorite Gewürztraminer from Chateau Ste. Michelle. A mistake as it turned out, he was a red wine guy. A Tower Records was located next to the wine store, so I bought him an instrumental New Age CD that I liked, *Conversations with God*. This resulted in a minor misunderstanding, namely that he thought I was a religious nut until I assured him that it was just soothing music that I liked to drive to. I left out the part that it cut down on my propensity for road rage. This guy had potential, and I wanted to keep him interested while I determined if I were interested. I also wanted to appear somewhat thoughtful, without looking blatantly conspiratorial.

State-Sponsored Sex

A year earlier I had dated a guy who introduced me to the Eastern Market, and in particular the signature dish served there on Saturday mornings, Blue-bucks, blueberry-buckwheat pancakes. When Mark and I arrived, the line for breakfast was out the door and snaking up 7th Street. I loathed standing in lines, but those pancakes were worth waiting for. The market buzzed with Capitol Hill residents and vendors. I looked around nervously, hoping my former boyfriend, who lived nearby, did not make an appearance. Our breakup had revealed a disturbing instability in his personality and a penchant for leaving long, weepy messages on my answering machine.

Mark looked like he stepped out of a J. Crew catalog, in faded jeans and a dark blue V-neck sweater with a white crew neck T-shirt peeking out. This outfit and his athletic build made him look a decade younger than his forty-nine years. The age-range criterion was looking more negotiable. Coincidentally, I was wearing a similar combination. I took that as a sign of our inherent compatibility. I started to take everything as a sign of our inherent compatibility.

As we stood in line, he hugged me and asked, "How are we doing?"

"Good, I think," I said, in what may have come out more as a question than a statement. Still, he did smell nice. His clean, fresh cologne mingled with the crisp autumn air.

After breakfast, I drove him back to his hotel, and he asked if I were free the following weekend. According to *The Rules*, I should have declined so as not to appear overeager or easily available, but quickly dismissed the thought, as I was certainly both. We began seeing one another every weekend. On my birthday, a little more than two weeks after his, he drove to Virginia in the middle of the week and took me to the Willard Hotel to celebrate. We had drinks in the Round Robin Bar, which used to be off limits to women, and dinner in their elegant dining room. Everything was going according to plan.

That was why I bought a house. After leaving the D.C. government, I relocated to Leesburg in order to cut my round-trip commute from two hours down to sixteen minutes. I despised apartment living but had not been able to locate a place to purchase that I liked and could afford. One evening after work, I discovered a pocket neighborhood of adorable town homes under construction in downtown Leesburg. They were designed in an antebellum style intended to complement and blend with the historic buildings of downtown. I stopped by the sales office and toured the available units. The agent told me a deposit of ten thousand dollars would hold my unit until construction was completed a few months later. I told the sales agent I needed to sleep on it. But really, my mind was made up, I just needed to call the bank and transfer money from my savings to checking. The following day after work I stopped by the office and dropped off a check for the deposit for my new home.

Did I think Mark and I had a future? I hoped so. However, the last thing I wanted Mark to think was that I was waiting for a guy to swoop in and rescue me from my life. My life was going pretty good; I did not need saving. And I was not going to put my life on hold, waiting to see what some guy was going to do.

Three weeks after our first dinner, I met Mark's mother, one of his sisters and an assortment of nieces and nephews. Beforehand, Mark and I decided to get our story straight. If anyone asked how we met, we were going to tell the truth. Neither of us saw the point in trying to hide the fact that we had met online. At dinner, I was seated next to Mark's sister, and she asked me, within the first few questions, how we met, and I told her, "Online." Her face registered surprise, but she quickly moved on with the conversation.

After dinner, I walked beside Mark's seventy-year-old mother on our way to our cars parked in the lot in front of the restaurant. Before getting into the car, she turned to me and, squeezing my arm, said, "I like you much more than those young stewardesses he usually dates."

I was happy that for once a mother seemed to approve of me. Later, when my elation wore off, I would obsess over her use of the word "young." Did she think I was old? I then obsessed over Mark's predilection for women employed in the aviation industry. Never mind that I did not exactly have stunning selection criteria, but his selection criteria were also those shared by most adolescent males.

A week later we flew to northern New York to celebrate Mark's best friend's birthday. His friends and their wives were cautiously friendly toward me. They had known Mark for more than twenty years. I sensed that I was one in a long line of Mark's female companions they had met over the years. Like parents during the Dark Ages, they were likely waiting to see if I would survive before making an emotional investment in me.

When Mark invited me to his place the following weekend, a stunned "holy moly" escaped my lips as I drove up the drive to his impressive lakeside home in the affluent Pompton Lakes area of northern New Jersey. This house was no primitive man cave. This place put the "man" in McMansion. I had never met anyone who lived alone in such a large house. He gave me a tour and was especially proud of his library that housed thousands of books, all of which he had actually read. I knew this guy was successful, but I did not realize just how successful until I saw his home. He received bonus points for good taste, a trait I likely cut when I was winnowing my criteria. His good taste, combined with exceeding expectations for the successful attribute, more than made up for him being slightly outside the preferred age range.

After dating for six weeks, Mark informed me he had been offered a job running a manufacturing company in

State-Sponsored Sex

China, and casually asked if I would go with him. I forced a laugh and said something indignant and uninspired like, "You can't be serious." I had recently landed the job of my dreams and was building a townhouse in Leesburg, Virginia. I had the comforts of small-town America with the amenities of the city a short expressway away. I was looking for a husband, not an exit strategy. The next time he brought it up I was more specific. "I'm not going to China as anybody's girlfriend."

"Well, of course not. That's not what I had in mind," Mark said when he broached the subject again.

What did he mean by that? I wondered, but left the question unasked.

Mark proposed to me, twice. The first time he proposed, he was talking about China and our future there as he prepared dinner for us at his home in New Jersey. Turns out he was also a good cook, another trait that was not on my list, but should have been. Since I thought I had been pretty clear that I was not moving to another continent just to keep dating, I used a passive-aggressive stratagem, one of the only ones in my playbook, to force the issue. I stalked out of the kitchen and slunk down into one of the overstuffed chairs in Mark's living room. He followed me out, wiping his hands on a kitchen towel, still susceptible to this stratagem. That would not last.

"What's wrong?"

"What do you mean, what's wrong? You keep talking about China and us, but I'm in Virginia, and you're leaving, so there's no us, there's just you." I was not making much sense, but if he noticed, Mark did not let on. He knelt in front of me and took my hands in his.

"Hey, I want you to marry me and move to China."

"Really?"

"I won't go unless you come with me. If you don't want to go, I'll keep my job here in New Jersey."

"Oh, okay." Now I did not know what I wanted. Did I want Mark and New Jersey or Mark and China?

The next time Mark proposed he did so on one knee with a traditional Tiffany diamond solitaire. I said yes without hesitation. My life was finally going the way I had always hoped. I had a job that was fun, challenging and paid well. The people I worked with, both my colleagues and my clients, were professional and interesting. My new home, located in a lovely and lively small town, was nearing completion. What the hell was I doing? Was it the romantic lure of an overseas adventure? Or was this the difficult, but reasoned decision that emerged after I weighed competing priorities? I followed a checklist, for chrissakes. He met the criteria, but place of residence and relocation ability were not on the list. I was forced to wing it. Even though I had almost everything, I still lacked someone to share my life with. I chose companionship over career and gave up my new community, job and friends. I have had it all, sequentially anyway.

State-Sponsored Sex

Before I embarked on my new life, I still had some mundane tasks in my old one to attend to. I cancelled the contract on my townhouse, losing my ten-thousand-dollar deposit. I gave notice at my job. When I did, my boss reminded me I had only been hired five months earlier. At the time, I had assured her settling in Leesburg and pursuing a career with Huthwaite were my plans for the future. Now I told her there would be other great jobs, but great guys were rare.

At that moment, all I knew was that I was being offered an unrepeatable opportunity to live in a foreign country with a wonderful man. An opportunity I thought would last a few years, and this was critical, at which time I would resume my paused career. Yes, I was making a long-term commitment to Mark, but only a short-term commitment to China. It was never my intention to give up my career. In fact, I thought the experiences and perspectives gained overseas would benefit my career. But sometimes effects or outcomes are not those predicted from purposeful action. I had no idea how quickly two years turns into ten, though my mother had been warning me for years, and all the twists and turns life takes during those intervening years.

Despite my ambivalence about having children, the Canon lawyer consulted by Fr. Jude, our Pre-Cana counselor, ruled that as long was I was open to the prospect of life our nuptials could proceed. After several weekend meetings preparing for the Sacrament of

Matrimony, Mark and I were married at St. Mary's Catholic Church in Pompton Lakes, New Jersey, June 10, 2000.

Did I owe my matrimonial success to Ellen Fein and Sherrie Schneider, co-authors of *The Rules*? In part, yes. True, I did break some of their rules. But, by instructing me to act as if I was a catch, Fein and Schneider convinced me to believe I was one.

FIVE

THE OTHER SIDE OF THE COMPASS

It was as though I had pulled the pin on a grenade, tossed it into my former life and then hopped in my getaway jet. A week after our wedding, Mark and I tapped his abundant cache of frequent flyer points and flew first class on Northwest Airlines to Hong Kong. My home and my job were gone. I sold my car and gave away all of my furniture. It was a pity there was no high-profile mobster trial for me to testify in because this was not bad for a do-it-yourself witness protection program. Hong Kong was more than eight thousand miles from New Jersey, and a parallel universe from El Paso, Texas and the Peking Palace restaurant.

A Mercedes sedan waited at the Hong Kong airport to transport Mark and me to our suite at the Excelsior Hotel in Causeway Bay. Arriving at the hotel, turbaned Sikh doormen greeted us at curbside and ushered us to our room. Growing up in a small town, I had dreamed of one day living in a big city. Now I found myself in one with seven million inhabitants, and it was exotic. For the first time, life was exceeding my expectations.

The Excelsior was our base during the summer of 2000 as we toured Southeast Asia. Mark acquainted himself with his company's operations in Asia Pacific while meeting his counterparts in other countries—all of this in preparation for taking over the company's Mainland China operations. I was adjusting to fluffy robes and daily housekeeping service. Beyond living the glamorous life, I had not envisioned what I would be doing in the big city. I was forced to improvise. Eat. Shop. Explore. Repeat.

Across Gloucester Road from the Excelsior Hotel, I discovered Jardine's Noonday Gun. In 1931 Noel Coward released the song "Mad Dogs and Englishmen," which references the heat of Southeast Asia and the gun, a naval artillery piece. Initially the Noonday Gun was fired in greeting at the arrival of the Jardine Matheson *taipan*. Taipans of old probably did stand on ceremony, but the gun may have also been a clever way of alerting the workforce that the boss had arrived at the office. I do not care how many stars it had on Tripadvisor.com, the gun was a dud.

I concurred with Coward on the hell-worthy heat. However, he claimed that only mad dogs and Englishmen went out in the midday sun. In Causeway Bay, I did see the occasional Englishman; however, still abundant throughout the day and late into the night were also Hong Kongers seemingly impervious to air

State-Sponsored Sex

that was both hotter and wetter than necessary. By contrast, I resembled a penitent, bent forward from the oppressive millstone of the Hong Kong summer heat, with copious rivulets of perspiration tracing courses down my back and chest. Eventually, I discovered the locals' secret, a cool reserve. It worked on the same principle as going inside in the winter to get warm and build up a reserve of body heat. In Hong Kong, the arctically chilled indoor air, unavailable in Coward's day, flash-froze the outer layers of the dermis, therefore buying me a few minutes of thawing time between the Excelsior and the Causeway Bay MTR station. It insured that my *arrectores pilorum*, the muscles that cause goose bumps, got a better workout than any other muscle group in my body.

At the Excelsior, a taciturn man named Peter oversaw the executive lounge, where I ate breakfast and developed the figure-wrecking habit of afternoon tea, complete with English scones, one of the few bright spots in the English culinary tradition. Peter possessed gravitas in inverse proportion to warmth and friendliness. Stepping into the lounge was like entering my own personal *Downton Abbey*, where Peter was my Carson. Some English traditions improved upon importation to America, governance, pies and oral hygiene. However, dry humor and moist scones were best left to the Brits. The Yankee version of a scone, a cross between a hockey puck and a doorstop, failed to make up in additional features, like chocolate chips or cranberries, what it lacked in moisture and buoyancy. In between meals, I worked off the scones in the hotel fitness center. I was not entirely successful. Those were tenacious little bastards.

My favorite lunch location became the Mandarin Oriental Hotel in Central Hong Kong. It was there that I would consume entire pots of fragrant jasmine tea that smelled like flowers and tasted like good health, long life and free radical devastation. I happily gorged myself on the dim sum offerings, steamed pork buns, turnip cakes and various other delightful pockets containing tasty combinations of shrimp, vegetables or fish. But the most appetizing discovery I made was the little round bun covered in sesame seeds and filled with a dark sesame paste. The buns were deep-fried to a gorgeous golden hue that yielded with a light crunch. They put fortune cookies to shame.

The limited time Mark and I spent together on weekends involved active pursuits like tennis at our hotel's rooftop court or hiking on one of the numerous trails crisscrossing mountainous Hong Kong Island. Mark loved to hike, and I gamely went along. On Stage 5 of the Hong Kong trail, near the Tai Tam Reservoir, Mark and I stopped for a break after walking up from Quarry Bay. This would have been a tough uphill slog under ideal weather conditions, but in the July heat, it was like doing hard labor on Mercury. Both of us were soaked through with perspiration.

State-Sponsored Sex

"Man, I am burning up. You must be dying under that rug of yours."

By rug, he meant my hair. The heat and humidity were making me peevish as it was, but this description of my crowning glory violated the unwritten code of newlywed decorum—diplomacy was supposed to supersede brutal honesty for a minimum of one year.

Prior to our wedding, and in anticipation of our relocation and travel schedule, I had my hair permed, thinking that it would be easier to take care of than my not-quite-straight but not-curly-either hair. This logical fallacy was notable due to its consistency and frequency. Every time I got perms, I assumed advances in perm technology promised better outcomes, curls like those depicted on a Rubens or Botticelli painting rather than on display at the American Kennel Club's annual dog show. In fact, perm solutions have changed little since the 1970s. Sadly, the combination of my inherited hair type, which inhabits the frizzy intersection between straight and curly, combined with the heated application to my hair of the acid glyceryl monothioglycolate and an average Hong Kong humidity of 87% in July resulted in deep-fried red tresses. All I needed was a bulbous nose and a honking horn to complete my clown college ensemble. Also notable for its consistency was that every time I had my hair permed I also told myself, *never again*. The following week I had my hair cut off above the shoulder, and mercifully the American Standard Poodle look went with it.

My ego was not only vulnerable to Mark's teasing. In those early months following our wedding and relocation to Hong Kong, I subjected myself to routine self-flagellation. When I accompanied Mark on a business trip to Kuala Lumpur, I began crying as I ran on the treadmill in the hotel's health club. As a Burt Bacharach festival broadcast from the Philippines played over the sound system, I listened to a vocal doppelgänger of Dionne Warwick croon "I say a little prayer for you," and I was overcome with unexpected sadness and loneliness. I missed the environment of work and the camaraderie of coworkers. Although I no longer had the pressure of project deadlines or demanding clients, I also lacked the satisfaction of accomplishment. Only a few months of adventure and already it was getting old. I tried to brush those thoughts aside. Surely any sane person would kill to be able to travel and sightsee full time. Buck up, I told myself. I needed to learn something else the Brits invented, the stiff upper lip.

I was not experiencing an enlightening, Oprah "Aha" moment. I was experiencing acute buyer's remorse. However, this was not a minor but ill-conceived purchase such as a pair of gladiator sandals, an Ed Hardy T-shirt or a Belgian waffle maker, this was a new life. What had I done? Sure, I was seeing the world, but with Mark working long hours, I was seeing it mostly by myself. Instead of a shared life, the only thing I seemed to be sharing was a bed and a bathroom, with a dude.

State-Sponsored Sex

After sharing a bathroom with five brothers growing up, it was a horror I had hoped to never relive.

I eagerly embraced the romanticized vision of the life of leisure while underestimating the satisfaction derived from the life of contribution. I held off sinking into despondency by assuring myself that, in just a few months, Mark and I would relocate to Shanghai, and there I would devote myself to worthy and rewarding endeavors.

SIX

....

CULTURAL DIVERSIONS

I possessed an inherited predisposition towards paranoia that living in China did nothing to diminish. By the time I relocated to Shanghai, I had lived and traveled to a few overseas locations with the air force, such as Japan, Germany and South Korea. I might not have known exactly what to expect in China, but I'd previously shed many of my preconceived notions about the lands beyond America's borders. The citizens of my new country of residence, however, were not completely used to seeing people like me. Foreigners, or *weiguoren*, were still objects of fascination on the mainland when I arrived in 2000. With red hair, blue eyes and pale skin, I may have been more conspicuous than most. Some of my neighbors said the attention made them feel like celebrities, but I always felt more like the bearded lady at a carnival freak show. Unlike me, at least the bearded lady got paid to be the object of curiosity.

To ease my entry into Chinese culture, my relocation company arranged a talk with a local historian when I arrived in Shanghai. Tess Johnston was originally from Virginia but had adopted Shanghai as her hometown. She was a local celebrity, having first arrived in Shanghai in the early 1980s with the U.S. Foreign Service. She remained in the city long after her retirement and meticulously captured in text and photography Western architecture and expatriate history in China. Tess was more Harper Lee than Paula Deen. Her silver hair was immaculately coifed, and a scarf accessorized her outfit, but her Southern-accented lecture was devoid of both political correctness and malice. When discussing the animosity the British-employed Sikh police force shared with the Vietnamese that served under the French, Tess remarked, "There was no brown brotherhood."

I met Tess at the Old China Hand reading room, a bookstore, tea and coffee house run by her literary collaborator, the photographer Deke Erh. Together they partnered on or published more than twenty-five books. For an hour, Tess regaled me with a condensed version of Shanghai expat history. Most of the stories were set in Puxi, in the same environs as the tea and coffee house we were seated in. We sipped strong, black tea in a room brimming with curiosities. Had Tess not been so interesting, my attention may have wandered to the antique treasures and books that surrounded us. Tess explained that Shanghai was once divided into concession territories belonging to several foreign powers. The Americans and British congregated in the

State-Sponsored Sex

International settlement, and the French had their own concession. According to Tess, the prevailing wisdom in old Shanghai was, "the Americans and Brits would teach you how to do business, but the French would teach you how to live." Nanjing Lu, formerly known as Nanking Road, was the dividing line between the International and French concessions.

In addition to the foreigners, Chinese fleeing competing warlords in the late nineteenth and early twentieth centuries swelled the Shanghai population. Although there was once a walled Chinese city, its walls were torn down early in the twentieth century. The Chinese population outgrew the tiny confines of the former walled city and expanded into the areas adjacent to the foreign concessions. Tess's talk intrigued me, and I was motivated to investigate Shanghai for myself. Thus began the first of my many attempts to set a course for myself while in China. Chinese cultural immersion, I decided, would be my raison d'être. As raison d'êtres go, it had a short shelf life.

With the help of detailed commentaries and gorgeous photos found within Tess's books, I discovered gems frequently overlooked by other visitors. One of my favorite discoveries was the last remaining section of the old Chinese city wall, Dajing Ge. It was usually deserted whenever I visited. I wandered the dark halls alone and gazed at the unlikely images of bats carved into the walls. In China, bats are an auspicious symbol. The Mandarin word for bat, *fu*, sounds like the word for good fortune. Because of this association, bat images are common design motifs and not merely Halloween decorations. Many cultural differences are subtle degrees of interpretation. I loved that this one was entirely opposite. I adopted the Chinese appreciation for the only mammal capable of flight.

Located on or near the Bund, the former premises of the HSBC bank, the former Peace Hotel and St. Francis Xavier Church were some of my favorite Shanghai buildings. Somehow I got away with wandering throughout the Peace Hotel, originally built by the Sassoon family and home to the Cathay Hotel until the 1950s. A few blocks down the Bund and hidden behind a high wall was St. Francis Xavier, which was built by the Jesuits and completed in 1847. When I peeked through the locked courtyard gate, a caretaker saw me and let me in. Although it was over a hundred and fifty years old, the small church was in good repair. St. Francis Xavier never made it as far north as Shanghai; instead he died in southern China in 1552, three hundred years before his namesake church in Shanghai was constructed. He was China's patron saint, whether they knew it or not.

On another solitary expedition, I visited what had once been a synagogue in the Hongkou neighborhood of Shanghai. This neighborhood was home to thousands of Jews during WWII. Shanghai was one of the few places in the world that did not turn Jews away and may have sheltered as many as thirty thousand during the war. When I visited the Ohel Moishe Synagogue, an elderly

Chinese caretaker let me in. I had never been in a synagogue before and had no idea what one was supposed to look like. I found large empty rooms with little ornamentation or furnishings. There were copies of old photos of the neighborhood taken during the war and depicting the Jewish community that lived there. The caretaker accompanied me as I viewed the photos, pointing out important features. He was friendly and talkative. He spoke English fluently and generously shared details of living and working in Shanghai's French concession prior to the war. He told me that he had worked in a French restaurant, and given his joie de vivre, I could picture him in a black beret with a baguette tucked under his arm.

"Where are you from?" he asked me.

"The U.S."

"Which state?"

"Texas."

"Oh, Texas," he said and turned serious. I braced myself for a President Bush comment, but he simply said, "Waco." I could tell from his demeanor that he was not a Baylor Bears fan. By "Waco," he meant the incident at the Branch Davic compound where many people, including children, had lost their lives in a federal government-led raid on the reclusive religious sect in 1993. Maybe this was his way of warning off inquisitive foreigners tempted to ask about Tiananmen, or perhaps it was an invitation to do so. I was not sure, so I finished looking around the synagogue and departed. As I sat in the car, I contemplated the unlikely historical vortex of Shanghai, Jews, WWII, French restaurants and Branch Davidians.

On another occasion, I requested that my husband's secretary, Sandy Tang, accompany me on a visit to Duolun Lu, a pedestrian street in Shanghai that had been home to several famous Chinese writers in the 1930s. We made our way down the street while Sandy translated some of the historic signs. I noticed she was becoming agitated, and I asked her what was wrong.

"I don't like history. I don't want to know what happened in the past."

I tried to explain that this was good history—nobody was killed. I mistakenly thought Sandy would find Shanghai's history as interesting as I did.

I was fortunate that these two incidents came so early in my tenure in China. As a result, I avoided controversial subjects that might embarrass or upset my Chinese hosts. The closest I came to broaching anything sensitive again was a conversation I had with a young tour guide in Kunming. As we visited an old temple near Dianchi Lake, I asked him what his religion was.

"My religion is me," he told me and then added, "and money. They are the only two things I can count on." Modern Chinese wisdom.

My cultural immersion project was doomed from the beginning, but it took me a while to figure that out. The primary reason it failed was that I do not blend anywhere on planet Earth. It was in China that I discovered I had a face that could make small children cry. After visiting Lake Tai, or Tai Hu, Mark and I stopped at a small grocery store in the town of Wuxi for something cold to drink. I was rounding the end of an aisle when I encountered a little boy playing with toys on the floor. He looked up at me, first startled, then frightened and began to wail. A woman materialized and scooped him up. I was mortified. Did she think I tried to harm her child? She gave no indication that she suspected I had done anything mean or unkind. Maybe like my Korean ex-boyfriend's mother, she took one look at me and also thought, "Those blue eyes, so ugly."

It was not only my eye color that set me apart. In China, I discovered a pre-tanning society, but just because I did not tan did not make us simpatico. I may not have mastered the Chinese language, but I knew what the phrase *bu hao* meant—not good. When several middle-aged Chinese ladies looked at me while saying "bu hao," I just knew they were zeroing in on my freckles. Asians like their skin pure white and blemish-free. Products promising skin lightening were prominently advertised throughout Asia. In addition to their ubiquity, these products were also notable for their marketing. They were unambiguously labeled "whitening cream." In most parts of Asia, dark skin and dark spots are beauty disasters. In China, with my red hair and sprinkling of freckles, I was esthetically disabled.

Until my departure from Shanghai in 2006, I remained a stare-inducing curiosity most places I ventured. I endured this public scrutiny long enough to see most of the top attractions in Shanghai and share them with the few guests who traveled to the Far East for a visit. As for my freckles, I never did like them, and now I felt my dislike was validated. One billion Chinese could not be wrong.

SEVEN

STEPFORD VILLAS

When I told Tess I found a place to live in Pudong, she remarked, "Pu-damn-dong?" Her face registered dismay and disappointment. Had I learned nothing from her Shanghai history lecture? I had moved from the country that invented suburbia to a Chinese version eight thousand miles away. Yes, Pudong was the burbs. Instead of steeping myself in the history and culture of Puxi, I chose a four-thousand-square-foot single-family residence with a garden and a carport located in a gated community. In my defense, with a forty-two-foot shipping container inbound from New Jersey filled to the brim with the contents of Mark's man-mansion, you bet I was looking for space.

By the time I arrived in 2000, Pudong was also home to a cluster of futuristic skyscrapers and wide, multilane roads that efficiently funneled traffic toward the multiple Huang Pu bridges or in the direction of the massive Pudong Airport. Before long it was home to two of the world's tallest buildings, the Jin Mao and the Shanghai

World Financial Center. Facing off on opposite corners, the Jin Mao reflected the elegant but edgy Gotham look while the Shanghai World Financial Center was a gleaming, futuristic sheath. At eighty-eight and one hundred one stories respectively, they stood emblematic of vertically oriented Asia. America felt horizontal by comparison.

A mere fifteen minutes' drive from the future was my own living time capsule from the past. Stepford Villas was the sobriquet conferred on my neighborhood by the expatriate community of Shanghai. The name alluded to a 1970s made-for-TV movie about a flawless neighborhood where housewives were offed by their husbands and replaced with look-alike fembots that were more submissive and gracious than their human models. The atmosphere of my neighborhood exuded a 1950s vibe, but with twenty-first century updates. Beehives and bullet bras were replaced with yoga pants and mobile phones. Stepford Villas was a time-warped neighborhood where the men worked and women made scrapbooks.

The appearance of the homes in my Shanghai neighborhood was similar to the cookie-cutter neighborhoods of boom-years Las Vegas, a vaguely Mediterranean palette with faux-tile roofs atop concrete rectangular structures. The uniformity of the homes and the precise landscaping were complemented by matching GM minivans in the driveways and stable nuclear families of four in each of the homes.

State-Sponsored Sex

The interiors of the homes in my neighborhood looked like an attempt at luxury by someone who had no idea what luxury was. The bathroom fixtures were gold-tone, but the bath and floor tiles were installed without skill or precision. The wood floors had buckled in places, and the basement frequently sprang leaks. Most disappointing, however, was the kitchen. Given my lack of culinary skills my concern about the kitchen was more esthetic than functional. In America, kitchens are often expensive centerpieces to a great room where the family gathered for quality time together. Throughout Asia, however, kitchens were typically cramped spaces behind solid doors. They were places for the domestic help to spend their time either in the task of meal preparation or simply to remain out of sight. Initially, we removed the door from our kitchen to try to open up the space. When kids came along, we put the door back up.

The Chinese government eventually lifted the restrictions on where foreigners could live, but when Mark and I arrived in 2000, they were still in place. Thus, our neighborhood was exclusively foreigners, mostly North American and European. Mark and I were the odd couple in the neighborhood. These were large, single-family homes, and we had yet to decide on the expansion of our family.

Returning from a stroll early one evening, Mark and I saw two women in front of the home next to ours. They stared at us but said nothing and made no movement to wave or greet us. Clearly they were not from Texas.

Mark was the nice half of the couple, so he suggested we cross the street and meet them.

"Hi, I'm Mark, and this is my wife, Claire."

"Hi," they replied, cautiously. We exchanged names and hometowns. They were both from Michigan, my suspicions were confirmed. They also had children, two each. They were surprised when we told them we did not. When I chimed in with our intention to get a dog, I was rewarded with tepid "ohs" and strained smiles. A few months later we adopted a cat who actively thwarted our charm offensive.

Miao Mao, which meant wonderful cat in Mandarin if pronounced correctly, which I likely did not, was an accomplished hunter and fisherman. It was the latter accomplishment that was not winning us any friends in the neighborhood. We assumed Miao Mao was snagging his fish from the neighborhood pond. We should have known better. That pond was stocked with koi and carp that were at least as big as he was. The dainty goldfish Miao Mao was bringing home were filched from the elegant ceramic fishbowls that were springing up on front porches throughout the neighborhood. The fishbowl trend was short-lived, probably due to Miao Mao's appetite. Eventually the supply of goldfish ran out, and Miao Mao returned to his usual diet of birds, which he consumed in their entirety, in front of me.

In the beginning, I was not too concerned that we did not seem to fit in at Stepford Villas. I was still getting to know Mark, so getting to know other people was not a priority. My other preoccupation was figuring out what to do with myself. It occurred to me that I was in an enviable position where I could ask myself, "If I could be anything in the world, what would I choose?" For several months, I was a full-time tourist, visiting every potential tourist destination in Shanghai. Over time, I would pursue other interests. Convinced failure was the only option, I eventually gave up trying to learn Mandarin. I dipped a toe into the world of genealogical research and got sucked in whole for life. It is, however, with profound relief that I managed to dodge the scrapbooking bullet. In reality, with minimal craft skills, it was never a serious threat.

EIGHT

STATE-SPONSORED SEX

Our visit to the sex-toy store was impromptu. I was intrigued by its unadorned window displays blatantly featuring dildos and vibrators and its bilingual sign that included the words "sex" and "health." It was located in the Puxi neighborhood of Shanghai, at the corner of Shaanxi Nan Lu and Julu Lu. Unlike similar establishments in the U.S., whose failed attempt at camouflage make them more conspicuous, this one was all clear glass and mirrors, with no attempt to disguise the merchandise. In America, sex-toy stores, even if they were located in dodgy neighborhoods, boasted wink-able names like the Smitten Kitten, Forbidden Fruit and Good Vibrations. By contrast, this store's bilingual sign seemed more appropriate for a medical office park: "The Huangang Sex Health Products Store."

Once inside, however, Mark and I were unable to blend into a throng of frisky locals, as there were none. We were the only customers and vastly outnumbered by middle-aged matrons in lab coats. Given the brightly lit and open configuration of the store, I felt as much on display as the merchandise. It was so orderly and antiseptic that it looked more like a pharmacy than a carnal superstore. There was definitely an air of medical necessity about the place. Instead of some burly guy with a beard and tats kicked back flipping through the latest issues of *Penthouse* or *Hustler*, the lab-coated matrons stood at attention looking like Chinese versions of Dr. Ruth. Upon closer inspection, the lab-coated ladies lacked Dr. Ruth's mirth and friendly demeanor. Instead, these ladies had the stone-cold expressions of prison guards. Not the kind of sex I had in mind. I kept my eyes averted and my head down. When we departed without making a purchase, it was hard to tell who was more relieved, the lab-coated matrons or my husband.

I have Sunday morning church service to thank for my discovery of the sex-toy store. When I arrived in Shanghai, I was still a consistent churchgoer. At the time, the only person I had to admonish for fidgeting was myself. Now with kids, well, let's just say I am in the religious reserves. Truthfully, part of me liked to attend church in China because for the first time in my life church attendance felt rebellious.

Knowing the government took a dim view of organized religion, in particular a Western import, made Sunday morning feel a little subversive.

I was really a faux insurgent because our church was, in fact, state-sponsored. We were establishment. Once or twice official-looking guys questioned the choir director

State-Sponsored Sex

and pianist, both Americans. We expressed outrage over this harassment but were secretly excited about it, as if we were starring in our own Robert Ludlum novel.

One of the paradoxes of China was oftentimes the lack of controls or regulations relative to the U.S., especially when it comes to zoning. For instance, this block was home to a church, a primary school, several residential apartment buildings and the sex-toy store. In America, sex has yet to emerge fully from the bedroom, so you will not find a sex-toy store next to Zara or the Gap at the local mall. Zoning Anywhere, USA, would never allow that. Ironically, today most sex commerce has moved online, which really means it has moved out of the bad part of town and into everyone's homes.

Mark resisted my entreaties to visit the store. I guess he was concerned that our driver, Mr. Chang, might think we actually had sex. To be fair, given its proximity to our church, neither of us wanted our fellow parishioners thinking the same. As Catholic Americans, we struggled with a powerful combination of Puritan rectitude and Catholic guilt. Sex was only sanctified if the objective was offspring, not getting off. However, one day we arrived early to church, so after getting dropped off by Mr. Chang and seeing him drive away, we walked back down the street to the sex-products store. Add deviant to subversive, and I started to see Sundays in a whole new light.

One of the lab-coated matrons explained to Mark that their products were for the disabled, those with unspecified medical conditions and single women, which I had not previously considered an affliction. I noticed several official-looking government certificates were framed and hung on the wall by the cashier, which I took to signify the store's government status. A dearth of customers also indicated that the store's funding stream came from somewhere other than actual sales. Admirably, the Chinese government deemed sex a medical necessity and established retail outlets to address this need, a refreshingly open view for a reputedly restrictive society. China's contribution to sexual health extends beyond its borders. Sex-toy consumers the world over owe a debt of gratitude to China, because according to the *China Daily*, 70% of the sex toys in the world are made there.

But was the Chinese government's message lost in translation? What were they trying to communicate, that sex was okay, even the government approves? In America, it was practically an article of faith that sex and illicit are meant to go together. When government and sex collide the result was usually a scandal involving interns, call girls or Instagram. Clean it up and make it official and all the fun deflates faster than you can say erectile dysfunction. Introducing state-sponsorship of an activity that goes by euphemisms like horizontal mambo, tube-snake boogie, and bump and grind not only diminishes the gravitas of the state-sponsored seal of approval, but also any shred of entertainment value the activity in question may have contained. Perhaps this

State-Sponsored Sex

was simply a bureaucrat's way of satisfying a central government edict of one-sex-toy-store-per-million-residents, with no intention of actually serving any customers or selling any merchandise.

In a newer neighborhood elsewhere in Shanghai, I encountered a different aspect of the Chinese sex industry. On a visit to my local bootleg DVD purveyor, who had recently moved locations, something he did regularly, I was surprised to see the street lined with barbershops, but then, that happens in China. In Shanghai, it was not uncommon to find similar businesses clustered together. So when my DVD guy moved, I assumed he had moved to barber street.

As it turns out, these were no ordinary barbershops. You may have gotten trim there, but never a cut. These were all brothels barely disguised as barbershops. In America, the red stripe on old-fashioned barbershop poles symbolizes blood because, in ancient times, barbers were also blood-letters. In China, brothels typically post a black and white pole. Red being the color of Communism would hardly look respectable connected with screwing, however apropos.

What was my first clue that it was not hair that was getting blown? There was not a sink or hair dryer in sight. Also, young women wearing clingy black dresses lounged around on couches. Like my DVD guy, the barbershop brothels made a meager attempt to appear legitimate, and that seemed to be all that was required to operate unmolested by the authorities. Unlike their government competition, they also appear to have found a business model that worked. The little black dress replaced the lab coat, and a modicum of privacy replaced the feeling of being in a sex-toy-store diorama. They were definitely onto something because, as opposed to their state-sponsored rival, these places were doing a bustling business.

If my visit to a Chinese state-sponsored sex store taught me anything, it was that the surest way to crush public interest in anything was not to ban it, but instigate a government takeover of it. The government's heart may have been in the right place, providing medical devices for the physical pleasure of the ill, infirm and single, but most people, regardless of political persuasion or nationality, do not want the government's hand in their crotch. Millions throughout the world privately appreciate that China has brought its manufacturing might to the sex-toy industry, even if it was not China they were thanking at the critical moment. However, the sex store's lack of clientele confirmed that I am not the only person that does not want the same organization that issues my driver's license selling me a vibrator.

NINE

CHINESE FIRE DRILL

Christine had rollers in her hair, and she and Carol were wearing pajamas, robes and wide, mischievous grins.

"Come on. We're going for a ride," Christine and Carol called to me from outside my bedroom window. It was the 1980s, and I was still in high school. Idling at the curb was Christine's family's car, a 1970s vintage Buick Estate station wagon in all its simulated wood-paneled glory.

"I'm going out the side door," I whispered as I grabbed my avocado green, quilted robe before tiptoeing down the hall past my parents' open bedroom door.

Back in those days bench seats were common in cars, and all three of us squeezed into the front seat. We were high school freshmen, and Christine's lack of a formal driver's education or a legal license did not deter us from embarking on an early morning road trip. We had no destination in mind, just happy to be wild and free before six in the morning. *Man alive*, I thought, *it is going to be a great day.* And from that moment, the act of driving was forever linked in my mind with the feeling of freedom.

Twenty years later, as a resident of the sprawling metropolis of Shanghai, I was chauffeured around town in a slinky, black Lexus ES 300. Door-to-door service wherever and whenever I wanted to go, that is, when Mark was not using the car. Mr. Chang was Mark's full-time driver supplied by his company. He was on a first-name basis with us, but we were not with him. When he was not transporting Mark to business dinners, client meetings, television interviews or factory visits, the Chang Man, as he became known to Mark and me in the most reverential way, was shuttling me around town for grocery shopping. He was our fifth and final driver. Our first driver quit to be a driver at an APEC summit, our second immigrated to France, and the others were fired. The Chang Man was the last man driving.

Mr. Chang loved our first car, a Lexus. China became the fastest growing market for luxury automobiles. However, in 2000 luxury cars were still relatively rare. The Lexus provided the Chang Man with performance, style and comfort, in addition to the respect paid to him by doormen and valets throughout Shanghai. Wherever he went in that car, he was immediately directed to a front-row parking spot. Not only did he operate his vehicle with speed and precision, he kept it immaculate. The other neighborhood driveways were home to GM

State-Sponsored Sex

minivans or worse, Volkswagen Santanas; only our driveway contained a luxury sedan.

In more than seven years of employment, he missed work only once, when he was hospitalized. He was so ill that Mark and I did not think he was going to make it. Thankfully, he recovered and was back at work, albeit considerably thinner, several weeks later. We never learned precisely what disease or condition felled him, but whatever it was, it was not enough to put a dent in his nicotine habit. Thanks to his cigarette smoking, the faint aroma of tobacco hovered around both the driver and the car. He had a jovial manner and a persistent smile; in fact, I rarely saw his face without one. Other than that, there was precious little I knew about the man. Communication between us consisted primarily of my survival Mandarin. This took the form of abrupt outbursts from the backseat of the car where I sat directly behind him, *zai nali* (over there), *ting, ting!* (stop), *metero* (the German version of Costco) and *port-o-man* (the Ritz Carlton).

After several months of being driven around town, the novelty began to wear off, and the slow-and-go traffic frequently made me carsick. I missed driving. After a little digging by my husband's executive assistant, it was discovered that foreigners could indeed get driver's licenses in China. Mr. Chang found my interest in obtaining a license amusing; in due course I would discover why. China did not offer reciprocal recognition of U.S. driver's licenses. Which meant, if I wanted to drive, I would have to pass their test.

The Chinese transportation department's licensing process for drivers involves a written and a practical exam. Fortuitously, I was provided with both the test of traffic laws along with the test answers, in English, which I studiously memorized. I was not sure if everyone was provided with such thorough preparation, but I was not complaining. During my initial driving exam in Texas, a state trooper sat in the passenger seat and evaluated my driving ability. His immaculate uniform and distinctive hat, combined with his formal demeanor, created an atmosphere of the utmost gravity. Taken together it had the effect of conveying the serious responsibility of operating a motor vehicle. In China, I would experience a practical exam that seemed more like a series of psychological experiments. This ominously foreshadowed the insanity of Chinese traffic.

In order to qualify for the practical portion of the test in America, a passing score on the written exam was typically required. In China, it was the other way around. Emphasizing driving skills over traffic laws might explain the casual regard most Chinese motorists seemed to have for traffic laws.

Mr. Chang accompanied me to the testing facility. Initially, I thought we were in the wrong place. The Shanghai version of the DMV office resembled a carnival. There was definitely a festive mood in the air. *Now this is cultural immersion,* I thought. I was given a

State-Sponsored Sex

check sheet indicating which rooms I was to visit. Each room contained a different examination. After successful completion of each task, I was given a "chop" or stamp, from the examiner. There was no particular order, but I had to complete and pass each one prior to being allowed to take the written exam.

I decided to ease into the testing process and started with the hearing exam, following that I proceeded to the vision test. In addition to testing basic vision, this test also revealed color blindness, which was grounds for disqualification. However, in China everything was negotiable. I saw customers try to negotiate the final amount at grocery checkouts. Therefore, it should not have been a surprise when the guy ahead of me failed the color-blindness test, he was not going to depart quietly. A negotiation ensued between the color-blind guy and the test proctor, and reinforcements were brought in from other testing stations to get the line moving again.

Next was the depth-perception test. Unlike hearing and sight, this was the first skills-based test. I sat at the end of what resembled a shuffleboard table. Midway down the length of the table was a two-by-four board with a notch missing, which bisected the table. Running the length of the table from the tester to the tested, and through the notch in the board, was a cable. Once I sat down and indicated that I was ready, the tester sent a target down the cable in my direction. I was supposed to press a button when the target passed through the notch in the two-by-four board. It seemed simple enough. Evidently Mr. Chang was not so confident in my abilities. He stationed himself beside the board with the missing notch, and as the target passed through the notch he began to gesture emphatically with outstretched arms. I was so surprised at his thrusting arm movements that I almost missed pressing the button. Collaboration was apparently tolerated, and the test proctor dutifully stamped my sheet before sending me on to the next station.

I may have failed the next portion of the practical exam because, frankly, I never understood it. For this task I stood in front of a spinning wheel about the size of a dinner plate that was covered with red dots. It was positioned about chest high. Above the dot-covered dinner plate was a steering wheel with two sets of needles pointing down towards the plate. The object was to guide the needles through, or around, the red dots. I was not sure which, so I simply wove my way around and through red dots until they told me to stop. The test proctor stamped my sheet, but only grudgingly. Mr. Chang seemed a little disappointed in me at that point.

One more skills test to go and a chance to redeem myself after my last performance. A large and boisterous crowd pressed into the doorway of my remaining driving challenge. I discovered that it was not the test that was so entertaining, but rather, the test proctor. A test taker sat at a table. Across the table from her was a standard traffic signal with red, yellow and green lights.

State-Sponsored Sex

There were buttons at each hand and a pedal under the right foot. The point of the test was to gauge reflexes and eye-hand coordination. Red light required pressing the foot pedal. The green light required pressing the right-hand button, and yellow light the left-hand button.

The current test taker was somewhat uncoordinated, so the test proctor was taking extra measures to assist her. The proctor had a long stick in her hand and was whacking the table next to the test taker's hand, indicating what button to press as the lights blinked on and off. All this whacking and the crowd's shouts and laughter had completely unnerved the test taker. Undeterred, the test proctor seemed resolute that no one was failing her test. She continued to whack away with her stick to roars from the crowd and frantic squeals and twitches from the test taker.

When the victim left, I was unclear whether she had passed or failed, but I did not have time to contemplate because Mr. Chang pushed me through the door and into the seat. The test proctor gave me a challenging look and explained in Mandarin what I was supposed to do. I nodded as though I understood, not because I actually did but because I did not want to give her a reason to start in with the whacking. Despite the pressure of the hungry crowd and stern proctor, I passed the test quickly and the stick was never used on me. The crowd, initially out for blood, cheered my success. Soon we would be adversaries on the road, but for a moment we savored each other's victories.

Despite my poor performance on the "driving wheel" portion of the practical exam, I was cleared for the written portion. I was anxious to proceed, as I did not know how much longer my short-term memory would hold up. I retained just enough answers to pass the test.

I was the proud recipient of a Chinese driver's license. I had a stronger sense of accomplishment after passing the Chinese driving test than when I got my Texas driver's license my senior year of high school. True, in Shanghai I never sat behind the wheel of a car with an impassive state trooper in the passenger seat. However, when I took the practical exam in Texas I never left second gear of my father's Honda Civic for the entire driving portion of the test.

A lot of good my new Chinese driver's license did me, because I never drove. The Chinese government may be authoritarian, but anarchists rule their roads. Driving across America from Los Angeles to Washington, D.C., including navigating through Hurricane Fran, was less daunting to me than the five-minute journey to the closest grocery store in my Shanghai neighborhood. I simply could not get the hang of uncontrolled intersections. Besides, if I had to keep my eyes on the road, I would be missing the rest of China. As much as I enjoyed the feeling of freedom I derived from driving, my desire for survival was greater. For the remainder of my time in Shanghai I left the driving to the professional, Mr. Chang.

TEN

I SAY DOUFU, YOU SAY TOFU

Growing up in a hunting family, in upstate New York, Mark swore they ate squirrel potpie as kids—one of the few things that sounded less appetizing than my mom's meatloaf, a dish even ketchup could not save. Friedrich Nietzsche may not have been thinking of food when he wrote, "That which doesn't kill you makes you stronger." That did not stop me from drawing strength from his philosophy whenever I was confronted with a challenging dining option in China. Having waited tables in a Chinese restaurant in high school, I thought I was well acquainted with Chinese cuisine. However, I discovered that most of the Chinese food served in America was Chinese in name only. Since my ability to cook was still an emerging skill in the early years of our marriage, Mark and I frequently ate out in Shanghai. Thus, I was afforded the opportunity to overcome my food aversions on an ongoing basis during my stay in China.

Shortly after our arrival in China, we visited the charming southern city of Kunming, famous as the home base during World War II of the Flying Tigers. While there, we were fêted by customers of my husband's company. It was a husband and wife business team. They owned a shopping center that had installed a panorama elevator made by Mark's company, the first of its kind in the city. They had recently opened a lakeside resort just outside of Kunming that we were invited to visit. The Chinese took tremendous pride in their rich culture, their cuisine in particular.

At dinner, members of the resort's management team joined us. We were seated at a large, round table. Mark was seated between the hosts. I was on the other side of the table flanked between people with whom I was unable to communicate. It was clear that I was on my own for that meal. So I smiled and nodded, a lot. A diverse array of dishes was placed in the center of the table on a large lazy Susan. I lost count of the number of dishes, but there were at least ten. The snacks arrived first—baskets of grasshoppers and what I thought were deep-fried worms. I snacked on the worms. With no legs or wings they looked like Cheetos, but without the cheese. They were more of a sensory input, all crunch and no flavor.

After our multicourse dinner, we were invited to a dance and music show featuring traditional songs and dances from the ethnic minorities that live in Yunnan

State-Sponsored Sex

province. On our walk to the theater Mark asked how I liked the dinner.

"I didn't mind the worms," I told him.

His face adopted a sympathetic expression normally reserved for disappointed toddlers. "Oh, sweetie, those weren't worms, those were deep-fried maggots."

Sure, it was a fine line, but worms being dirt eaters seemed a little less revolting than the larva of flies, an insect weaned on shit.

Other than our hosts and their managers, we were the only people present at the show. I was awed by the effort that had been expended on our behalf. But the evening was not over. After the show, we were escorted to a lakeside BBQ pit. There our host grilled mushrooms for us. Yunnan province has many varieties of edible mushrooms. I had never eaten grilled mushrooms before, or since. These tasted both earthy and smoky and were delicious. That we were eating them around a grill under a starry sky made it a tasty end to an enchanted evening, almost. Maggot consumption was not forgotten, but it was forgiven.

Thankfully, it was not all fungus and insects. Despite the fact that little of what I encountered in China resembled anything from the Peking Palace restaurant back home, I did really like some of the things I ate. One of my favorite Chinese dishes originated in Sichuan province, it was called *mapo doufu*. The translation of this delicacy conjured images better suited for the dermatologist's office than the dining room. Mapo doufu means pockmarked lady's tofu. If you could get past the title, it was a delicious, spicy tofu dish.

Mapo doufu was not to be confused with stinky tofu, which, of course, I did. Stinky tofu was a fermented tofu dish with a pungent odor. The first and only time we ordered that dish, Mark took a healthy bite, motivated by my glowing reviews. After doing so his face tightened, he chewed quickly and swallowed with effort. After a long pull on his Tsingtao beer, he insisted that I eat a bite too. I would have tried it anyway, just out of curiosity. I decided that stinky tofu, along with Nature Valley Granola Bars, would likely only be palatable in the event of a zombie apocalypse when foods stores begin to run dry.

The different cuisine was not our only dining challenge in China, customer service was the other. In the neighborhood Mark and I moved to, we encountered a restaurant that actively discouraged customers. Faced with an empty refrigerator on our first night in our new home, we decided to walk to the restaurant located inside the neighborhood clubhouse. It was devoid of customers, and the staff gathered in the kitchen seemed surprised to see us when we wandered back there looking for service. That was the first hint to find an alternate dining option. The second hint was served in the form of fried lettuce, the daily vegetable option. What the estate agent had failed to mention when we toured the neighborhood was that the restaurant was used exclusively to prepare meals for the neighborhood construction workers. When we moved in, the development was only half complete. A few years later, and after the construction was finally completed, a lovely restaurant that served more than lettuce did eventually move in.

As dismaying as the menu in real Chinese restaurants may be to those raised on American Chinese food, consumption of other cuisines in China was not without peril. I learned the hard way that restaurants offering anything other than Chinese food in China, like Mexican or French, for example, required careful scrutiny to insure that a foreigner who matched the cuisine really did work in the kitchen. Failure to do so resulted in food approximations, like quiche made without eggs, pita bread passed off as pizza and enchiladas with red curry sauce. When I tried to bring the discrepancy to the attention of my Shanghai waitress, I did not get attitude, just impassivity.

While in China, Mark and I held a nearly unbroken streak of confronting and consuming culinary challenges. There were two notable failures. First was the turtle. I just could not do it. It reminded me of the old box turtle that showed up from time to time in our backyard as a kid. My husband was less susceptible to sentimentality. He nonchalantly sliced off its head and mucked it on down. But even Mark had a limit to his eating envelope. When offered a donkey dong, he politely declined. He later explained it had something to do with gender solidarity.

Dining options in Shanghai in 2000 were meager, and my culinary skills nonexistent. Mark brought a library of cookbooks into the marriage, but I only brought one, *The Joy of Cooking*. I had been lugging it around for years without ever actually opening it. After arriving in China, I began studying that book, because, unlike many cookbooks that provide little more than recipes and a few shiny photos, the Rombauer sisters provided the essential kitchen education I missed when I skipped home economics in high school. My cooking slowly improved along with the selection and quality of international restaurants in Shanghai. In just a few years, Shanghai became known as something of a culinary hub in Asia. At the same time, my kitchen prowess increased thanks to the Rombauer sisters. I guess Nietzsche was right. Despite an intense bout of self-inflicted food poisoning from an expired can of tuna, Mark and I were both still alive. And while there were many nights Mark came home to a dinner consisting of refried beans smeared on corn tortillas, he and I survived both my home-schooled cooking education and the nascent Shanghai restaurant scene.

ELEVEN

REALLY DESPERATE HOUSEWIFE

When my college roommate Andrea explained to me that her life plan was to get an accounting degree, work for a few years at a great job and then quit to become a housewife, I stared at her like she was a traitor to her gender, with two heads. Raised in post-Betty Friedan America, the women of my generation were never supposed to be housewives.

When did people start asking children, "What do you want to be when you grow up?" I doubt that question was ever asked of my grandmother. Until the last century, it was not a question anyone would think to ask because the answer would have been a foregone conclusion. A woman's place was in the home. But in the latter half of the twentieth century, women's choices expanded beyond teacher and nurse. For some single-minded individuals the answer may have been invariable from a very young age. As a child, I rarely answered that question the same way twice. To be clear, my primary motivation was not limitless choices but, rather, fear.

Fear that I would pick the wrong career and be stuck in a sucky job for life.

In second grade, I wanted to be a singer and an actress. At YMCA day camp that summer I received the award for best actress, and loudest singer. I suppose with volume comes distortion. My father restricted my television viewing to news programs and PBS documentaries. This was during the pre-cable era, so I was not really missing much. As a result, by junior high I developed an interest in broadcasting, specifically investigative reporting. Like acting and singing, an audience was still involved. As the youngest in a large family, attention was hard to come by and likely shaped my decision making. In my old copy of *Free to Be... You and Me* I discovered an assignment from my seventh grade English class tucked inside the front cover. In it, I write that I want to be a television journalist, like Geraldo Rivera and Barbara Walters. At the time, both were on the television news program 20/20, Walters as host and Rivera as one of the show's intrepid reporters. Walters has since moved to *The View* and Rivera to the lunatic fringe.

I may have forgotten that bygone aspiration had I not found my childhood book and took a moment to look through it. I have wanted to be many things, more than I have actually been, but I have managed to be a lot. Some of my occupations sounded better than they really were. Air force intelligence officer sounded like martinis and sports cars, but it was really humid vaults with

State-Sponsored Sex

mushrooms growing in the carpet. Some of my occupations were as bad as they sounded: substitute teacher, cleaning lady and tamale server. I may not have known exactly what I wanted to be, and I may have been haphazard in my career progression, but it never occurred to me that I might one day be a housewife.

Initially, my use of the term housewife was reluctant and compelled. Every time I returned to China, I was required to fill out the immigration form the flight attendant handed me. Although I was newly married, it was not the unfamiliar last name I stumbled over, but the request to identify my occupation. When asked about how they completed the immigration paperwork, the other neighborhood wives told me they wrote in fictitious occupations. That struck me as a really bad idea when entering an authoritarian country. It was not that I cared what the immigration officer at Pudong International Airport thought. The term clashed with my own perception of myself. I simply did not see myself as a housewife, but I was coming up empty on any other appropriate descriptive term. Thus, every time I crossed the Pacific or returned from elsewhere in Asia or Europe, I grudgingly filled in "housewife" on my immigration form.

Mark seemed a little disturbed by this title, as though he had not fully considered the ramifications of our change in status from dating to married. He was already prepared for my financial dependency; what he did not calculate was my identity dependency. The authors of

The Rules urged me to be an intriguing woman like no other but left me in the lurch once they got me down the aisle. Without my successful career, I felt exposed and vulnerable. It was as though I no longer knew how to describe myself. And the words that did readily come to mind I did not like. I did not simply change my marital status when I relocated to China; I stepped back in time. I went from being a modern career woman (even that term sounded obsolete) to a 1950s-era housewife in the space of a transpacific flight.

However, the timing of my entrance into the domestic career force was impeccable. The title "housewife" was on its way out. It had ceased to be a descriptor and instead become a pejorative. Housewife might have gone the way of "stewardess" and "secretary" were it not for the efforts of two gay men working independently to resurrect it. Thanks in part to Andy Cohen, the creator of *The Real Housewives* franchise on Bravo TV, and Marc Cherry, the creator of *Desperate Housewives* that appeared on ABC, housewives were back in vogue. Their use of the term combined with the propagation power of the Internet unleashed a diverse populace of housewives that were Pakistani, holistic, dirty, accidental, drunk and hot. Hillbillyhousewives.com, frugalhousewives.com and reluctanthousewives.com all fought, not for the best pie recipe, but for search engine optimization.

However, I still discovered that when I mentioned my occupation as a housewife it was a conversation ender, not opener, because people thought they knew what I did. They thought they do the exact same thing after work and on the weekends but simply did not consider it a career choice, and it was not just my sister. Living overseas, however, I was not like other housewives. In China, women like me were referred to as *tai tais*. The term was initially used to describe the first wife in a polygamous marriage. It evolved to describe wealthy, married women with excess time on their hands who rarely rose before nine o'clock.

Having been raised solidly middle class in America, I did not initially identify myself as wealthy and privileged. The fact was, I was not wealthy, but I was an expat. Expats lived in and visited places most Americans would have trouble locating on a map. The expat lifestyle in China was a departure from life in America. The same advantageous wage structure that denuded the American landscape of manufacturing jobs in favor of cheap Chinese labor allowed American expats in China to hire housekeepers, nannies, drivers and masseuses that made house calls. The housewives of my neighborhood did not have to concern themselves with the mundane tasks of domesticity because they could outsource them, even if they did not want to admit it. I know I didn't.

In the early years of our marriage our socializing involved fine dining and good vintages; later, it was more likely to involve jumpy castles and chicken nuggets. Back then cooking and entertaining other people was a treat, not part of my daily duties. Mark especially liked having colleagues over for dinner so he could display his grilling skills. Even as a bachelor he did a lot of cooking. With feeble cooking skills, I was usually relegated to a support position when company came over—like making sure the powder room had toilet paper.

After a particularly successful dinner, one of our guests complimented me on the meal. When I explained to her that Mark did all the cooking, she cocked her head and loudly asked, "Then what do you do?" Truth was, not a whole lot. My *ayi*, Xiao Yin, did the cleaning and laundry. That did not prevent me from being slightly offended. I preferred to think of myself as on sabbatical, but her question made me feel like a freeloader.

When I was asked, "Do you have servants in your home in China?" by an African-American flight attendant on a United flight from San Francisco to Shanghai, I stuttered and stammered an embarrassed, "Uh, yes, a housekeeper and a driver." Later, at an international expat's luncheon in Shanghai, a woman from India accurately observed, "Americans are the only people I know embarrassed to employ domestic help." I did not put much effort into the position of housewife because I thought it was a temp position. That I was outsourcing most of the work was just as well.

TWELVE

RUB ME THE WRONG WAY

Without the inconvenience of actual housework to perform, I morphed into a hybrid "Stepford" cum "Real" housewife, occupying my time with activities such as cooking classes, luncheons and working out. Before dropping Mark off at his office in the morning, Mr. Chang would deposit me at the Shanghai Hilton, where I would spend my morning exercising in the hotel's health club. However, my favorite way to spend my time was at one of the many new spas springing up throughout Shanghai. On the surface this would appear to be an entirely self-indulgent endeavor, yet through it I gained interesting, if at times painful, insights into other cultures. Eventually, I in-sourced my massage habit. This resulted in a more consistent experience, but one that was less culturally illuminating.

My exposure to the hedonistic world of spa ministrations began accidentally when I was still in the air force. On a cultural tour to Gyeongju, South Korea, subsidized for service members by the Korean-American

Friendship Association, I was initiated into the world of spa indulgence. Prior to checking in at a swanky Gyeongju resort, I toured what was described as the "Santa Fe of Korea." No adobe dwellings or turquoise jewelry, but lots of headless Buddha statues. Apparently when Confucianism supplanted Buddhism in Korea in the fourteenth century, heads rolled.

My Korean cultural and educational obligations fulfilled, the first item on my weekend agenda was a visit to the ladies' spa. It was cavernous and damp with apple-shaped Japanese retirees milling about in matching black maillots as though it were a Lands' End catalog shoot. In plain view of everyone were two massage tables. Two masseuses stood at the ready. Unfamiliar with the world of massaging, it did not occur to me that this was in any way unusual, but the masseuses were both clad in lacy lingerie. Another service member on my tour, Kim, saw me eyeing the tables and suggested I give it a try. I hopped up on the damp table, which was apparently hosed off between guests. I was promptly coated with a generous portion of oil. The term portion was not accidental as the oil had a faintly culinary scent that I eventually put my finger on. For the next hour, a lingerie-clad masseuse rubbed me with sesame oil. *Was this how human sacrifices were prepared before being tossed to the ravenous Aztec gods?* I wondered. The richly scented air, the pounding and kneading, and let's not forget, the gathering audience looking on in anticipation. The experience may have been shared, but it was no less pleasurable.

Initiated into the world of spa indulgence, I was eager to partake upon a subsequent trip, this time during my next air force assignment to Japan. I did not have to look hard to find a bathhouse—Japan was famous for them. I checked in at one not far from my apartment.

Bathhouses are more than merely public hot tubs. They are entertainment complexes that just happen to be centered on being clean. Leaving the bathing area for one of the other entertainment options, such as video, gaming, eating or massage, patrons don cotton pajamas. These pajamas were light blue and sprinkled with stars. They were pressed and comfy. I padded around the halls in slippers, smiling at my co-bathers dressed in identical pajamas. Everyone appeared happy and sedate as if we had all just taken our meds. Some people sat in electric massage chairs located in sunny atriums. Others dined in the café. And for the adventurous, there was the karaoke lounge.

I followed the siren call to the massage room. Similar to my Korean experience, the massage beds were communally located. I grew concerned, as there seemed to be no gender segregation. I need not have worried. Pajamas were not to be removed, and additional towels were draped over me so I resembled an accident-scene victim—foreshadowing as it turned out. When I arrived only one other table appeared occupied. It was a large lump of towels being worked over by another masseuse.

My masseuse pointed to a bed, and I obediently climbed up and laid face down.

Apparently I am not as culturally relativistic as I aspire to be. Relief of sore or stressed muscles may be the intent of massage in some places, but perhaps not all. I had signed up for shiatsu massage. It belatedly occurred to me that shiatsu sounded disturbingly like "she assault you," which, it turned out, was not far from the truth.

I wistfully recalled those oily, scantily clad Korean ladies the entire time Tojo was avenging her ancestors on my back. At one point, I wondered if she had called in reinforcements. There were simply too many things touching me at once. It was then I realized she was on top of me, working me over with her bony knees and tiny hands. At another point, I thought she was gouging me with a broom handle, only to realize it must have been her elbow. But no, in case you are wondering, I did not cry out. Whoever was on the other table did not utter so much as a grunt. I would not be the first to break. The only sound I made was the sigh of relief when the towel was pulled back, indicating I had survived and was being released.

Chastened by my Japanese experience, I swore off massages for several years. Arriving in Shanghai, I noticed "blind man" massage establishments found throughout the city. I learned later that while some of the masseuses are blind, many were not. My experience involved a masseur who had his eyesight. This turned

State-Sponsored Sex

out to be a big mistake. I learned afterwards from other blind-man massage veterans that sighted masseurs were to be avoided due to their overzealous devotion to their trade. This guy made Tojo seem like Hello Kitty. Instead of massaging muscles, this guy was targeting bones and joints. One of us was in the wrong place. I was trying to get a massage, and this guy was trying to force a confession.

Every few months Shanghai seemed to add another five-star hotel with a de rigueur spa. Visiting the "it" spa of the moment, I was offered a menu of massage choices from a variety of countries. I decided to try something ancient and exotic. My exotic massage consisted of a stream of oil poured onto my forehead. Far from transcendent, or even relaxing, I left that massage with what looked like a third red eye in the middle of my forehead. I avoided human interaction until the eye disappeared, sparing me the embarrassment of admitting to a massage injury. During another massage, the masseuse rubbed my chest, yes, my entire chest. It did not feel bad, just wrong. Still another young woman remarked while she was rubbing my legs, "You have a very beautiful bottom." That was before I had children.

When the in-home massage trend hit my Shanghai neighborhood, I was an early adopter. A neighbor finagled a second shipment of household goods from her husband's company and stocked the shipping container with massage tables from Costco. She sold them to neighbors at cost. Soon the trendiest homes in the neighborhood boasted personal sanctuaries of tranquility and supple muscles. The neighborhood shared the same masseuse, who provided both one- or two-hour massages. I decided two hours were too decadent and only booked one hour. I even provided my own oil—sesame.

Still, it was not something I bragged about to family in the States. The need for a driver was explainable—foreign country with different driving customs. A full-time housekeeper less understandable, especially with only two people in the household at the time, but not too outrageous. But a masseuse that made house calls? What next, a personal grape peeler? No, that detail would remain dormant only to reemerge as a delicious little irony that would haunt me for years to come when I assumed the duties formerly performed by Xiao Yin and Mr. Chang. In that dystopian future, my long-suffering back would cry out for relief, but my schedule would be lucky to accommodate sufficient sleep.

THIRTEEN

BEAUTY SCHOOLED

My love of the spa life clouded my judgment, or maybe the aromatherapy went to my head. After a year and a half in China, I decided to return to the U.S. for beauty school. What did Mark think of my idea? He never said. I chose the manicure program not because the answer to the question, "If I could be anything, what would I be?" was manicurist. I chose the manicure, or nail technician, program after careful market analysis. Despite the explosion of spas around town, there were few nail salons in Shanghai at that time. Also, the manicure program was the shortest and cheapest. And to be honest, polishing nails had a limited potential for damage. Polish could be retouched in the event of a smudge. However, give a woman a bad haircut and she would be miserable for weeks, maybe longer. She would also spread hate for you far and wide.

The plan was to finish the program in the minimum time required—six weeks. Following successful completion of my nail tech program, I needed to pass my state licensing exams, a written exam and a practical demonstration of skills. I honestly believed I could complete the program and tests and return to Shanghai in less than two months. Thanks to the exam schedule and two brief but intense illnesses, a ceviche-induced bout of food poisoning and a debilitating reaction to hair dye, I did not return to Shanghai for three months.

With the largest concentration of my family members located in Las Vegas, I chose a school located in that city. My primary motivation was a free place to stay at my brother Danny's house. Danny was both a nice guy and an aerospace engineer. Therefore, I expected him to say yes when I asked if I could stay with him, but also I expected him to be single. I was right about the first, and wrong about the second. He could not turn me down because one, I am family, and two, he was nice. His girlfriend, however, was happier at my departure than my arrival.

I selected the Academy of Beauty based on their web page. Photoshopping, I discovered, was not limited to aging celebrity faces. Online, the Academy looked like a pleasant place to learn with motivated students enthusiastically polishing nails and snipping bangs. In person, the Academy more closely resembled a prison visitation room, with grim-faced people staring at one another across pitted and scarred tables while discussing antisocial behavior in hushed tones.

Remorse was becoming a chronic condition with me. I wanted to quit as soon as I arrived, but could not bring myself to do so. I did not want to admit to Mark that I had made a poor choice. I decided to gut it out at the Academy, no matter what. Over the coming months, I endured a Cuban guy who thought he was Tony Montana and communicated almost exclusively by quoting lines from *Scarface*.

After microwaving my frozen Amy's cheese enchilada lunch in the school break room, he loudly declared to the entire school, "Someone cooked fuckin' shit in the break room."

"These are Amy's organic, gluten-free enchiladas." I was indignant. "And they're far more nutritious than that fast food you're eating." Ooo, I had him now.

"Yeah, well, this is fuckin' organic too." Yeah, like I really believed him.

Then there were the two hair design students whose dispute over a styling station came to blows right next to my manicure and pedicure station. Teachers broke up the melee before they knocked over my polishes. They were suspended for a week. A manicure student who started with me quit in a huff after she was criticized for filing the top of a customer's foot while the elderly woman suffered in silence but writhed in agony.

From the beginning there were obvious signs I attempted to ignore that the Academy was not the thriving esthetic academic center it purported to be. The school operated out of a desolate, and mostly unoccupied, strip mall. Along with a bar and a Mexican food restaurant, it was one of the only remaining tenants in a retail center in decline. The boarded-up facade of a former discount retailer stood like a gaping economic wound on the opposite side of the L-shaped center. On a positive note, there was always plenty of parking available. The Vegas neighborhood the strip mall was located in had even less personality than Pudong, but just as many questionable drivers.

Despite decades in operation, the Academy had a low-cash-flow, startup-enterprise look about it. Seats in the classrooms and the school salon were metal folding chairs. Supplies were cheap and generic. The students resembled a meeting of the UN, if the UN was comprised mostly of strippers. An aging lesbian couple taught the manicure and esthetician programs. Their leathery faces the result of years of baking in the unforgiving Nevada sunshine and their colossal consumption of cigarettes. What their faces did not reflect were regular facials or proactive anti-aging interventions.

In addition to providing instruction on manicures, pedicures and artificial nail enhancements, our nail technician instructor included tax evasion as an additional bonus. She instructed us to keep two ledgers, an accurate one for ourselves and a more modest accounting for the Internal Revenue Service. Her teaching ability was as dodgy as her integrity. But if her math skills were anything like her personal grooming, the I.R.S. would be unlikely to ever get accurate numbers out of either of her ledgers.

State-Sponsored Sex

One of my classmates was an unstable Iranian—a condition that had apparently spread from the government to some of its citizens. She occasionally attended class, but even then she was prone to outbursts and dramatic exits if anyone disagreed with her or criticized her work. My classmates, unconstrained by the tethers of political correctness, called her bat-shit crazy. As the youngest of seven children, I was familiar with the role of outcast and frequently came to her defense. Unfortunately, this earned me a seat next to her at our state board written exam. She tried to cheat off my test and became quite agitated when I would not cooperate. I did not help her because I had no desire to get caught. I really wanted to get home and was behind schedule as it was. Besides, there were multiple versions of the exam. Even if I had supplied her with answers, they would not have helped her because it was highly unlikely that she and I possessed the same version of the test. I patiently, but futilely, tried to explain that to her after the exam. When our test results arrived at the school a week later, I passed, but she failed and blamed me.

Once I passed the written exam, I applied to take the practical exam. Since I had to demonstrate the ability to perform a manicure and sculpt acrylic nails, I needed a model for the test. My sister agreed to be my willing victim. Unfortunately, the earliest available test was scheduled in Reno. If I wanted to get back to Shanghai as soon as possible, I needed to go to Reno, a dumpier version of Vegas with a better climate. Our round trip to

Reno was completed in less than twenty-four hours. I had to wait for the test results to be mailed, but I was confident I passed the test.

Eager to get started, I packed three large suitcases with the supplies necessary to run a small nail salon. Upon my return to Shanghai, all I needed to do was unpack my polishes and advertise my new venture, Fu Fu Nails. I thought I had the elements necessary for success. I was conveniently located in a large neighborhood. I had both training and quality materials. What I did not carefully consider—price point. Women were willing to pay a lot for their hair and as little as possible for their nails. The economic downside of "limited potential for damage" I had not previously considered.

FOURTEEN

SHOCKED UP

I do not know what got into Mark. Was he concerned that my successful completion of vocational training expanded my horizons to the point of jeopardizing our marriage? When we married, I thought we had both been ambivalent about children, so much so it actually imperiled our nuptials at St. Mary's Catholic Church. Only when I agreed that I was open to the possibility of life did the Canon lawyer relent. However, upon my return from Nevada, Mark began actively lobbying to start a family. Did I miss a wink and a secret handshake between him and the men in white collars?

"Look," I cautioned him, "given our age it will likely take nine to twelve months to conceive." *And with any luck*, I thought to myself, *maybe never.*

Besides, I had every intention of embarking on my entrepreneurial career. I returned to China and promptly framed my manicurist license from the Nevada State Board of Cosmetology. I carefully organized my exotic rainbow of nail polish and set up my home salon. I naively thought in the unlikely scenario that I became pregnant anytime soon, I would be able to do both. That was supposed to be the point of a home-based business, or so I thought.

Why was I resistant to motherhood? Unbeknownst to Mark, I continued to fail all my self-imposed litmus tests to determine suitability for motherhood. The toughest hurdle was the Janelle Test, named for my sister-in-law. It was not only Janelle's Texas accent that was sweet; she oozed niceness. Parental discipline Janelle-style undoubtedly involved hands on hips, arms akimbo and a stern but simultaneously loving look. Could I ever be that kind of mother? Not a chance. I also failed the cuter species question. When confronted with the choice of what was more adorable, puppies or kittens, I was indecisive. But compare either to actual human babies and I was no longer an ally of my species.

So when I began to feel sick, pregnancy was not the first thing to come to mind. I thought it was another bout of food poisoning coming on, a misery I actually welcomed. I had started to gain weight, and there was nothing like a few days of vomiting and diarrhea to drop five pounds and curb the appetite, brutal but effective. After a few days, it felt more like a trend than a bout. Payback, I suspected, for ignoring the advice to stick with an ox or a rooster and mating instead with a rabbit. Perhaps this was not the best time to confess to my husband that the only job I had ever been fired from was as a nanny.

State-Sponsored Sex

Prior to meeting Mark for drinks at the Shanghai Ritz-Carlton, I purchased a pregnancy test from the grocery store adjacent to the hotel. I took it to a small bathroom tucked away on the second floor that only regulars knew about. I knew I would need a minute for the stick to develop and did not want to proceed in a crowded bathroom. As I had hoped, I had the place to myself. I waited for what I expected would be a negative test. The result, however, was positively surprising.

"Your hair looks nice," my husband said as he stood up to kiss me when I entered the bar. I warned him that morning I was getting my hair done, and he reciprocated by noticing. "What would you like to drink?"

"A ginger ale," I said, eliciting a Spock eyebrow from Mark at the nonalcoholic request. He motioned for the waiter and placed my drink order. He was already working on a Bombay martini.

I was freaking out and susceptible to melodramatic impulses. I said nothing as I pulled the pregnancy test stick from my purse and slid it across the table. My husband stared at the stick for a moment, not sure what he was looking at.

"Is it mine?" he asked, after comprehending its significance.

"No, it's the fucking cat's. Was that supposed to be a joke? Because it sucked."

"Oh, come on, where's your sense of humor?"

"Apparently MIA, like yours."

Mark fucked up one of my life's significant moments by trying, and failing, to be funny. That he was attempting humor at my expense made this an unforgivable crime, for which he continues to do penance. It was not as if I would have numerous opportunities in the future to make a similar announcement. I was no Michelle Duggar or Octomom. Besides, there would never be a first child ever again. Announcing a wanted pregnancy ranked up there with college acceptance and a marriage proposal in terms of life's biggest news.

For the next few months we kept our big news to ourselves. Combating morning sickness was my full-time occupation, and it came at the expense of my nascent manicurist career. I tried acupuncture, which worked, but only for a few days; then I would need to return to the acupuncturist to spend another hour as a human pincushion. I found a bracelet that used acupuncture principles to stimulate the medial nerve and thereby calm the stomach. It worked, so I wore it continuously for the next three months.

I thought about returning to the U.S. to give birth, but could not find an obstetrician there that would take me on as a patient. Unless I was willing to return to the U.S. for the duration of my pregnancy, no doctor there wanted anything to do with me. The best they could do was suggest that I return to America in my last trimester and then present myself at an emergency room when I went into labor. Maybe it was the influence of too much

State-Sponsored Sex

Grey's Anatomy, but I didn't want a gunshot victim bleeding out on one side of me and an incurable disease on the other as I pushed a vulnerable new life into the world.

Instead, I looked to Hong Kong and found a doctor and a hospital I was comfortable with. When I met my obstetrician, who came highly recommended, he looked like a twelve-year-old. I assumed he was some kind of wunderkind—like an Asian Doogie Howser. Months after my son was born I worked up the nerve to ask Dr. Lam his age. When he told me he was forty-three, I silently cursed my genetic shortcomings and started drinking more green tea, knowing even as I did so I was decades too late.

The Matilda Hospital, a Hong Kong institution dating back more than a hundred years, sat atop Victoria Peak and resembled a luxury hotel. I just knew giving birth there was going to be great, as long as my taxi could make it past the line of tour buses snaking their way up to the Peak.

My new condition meant my entrepreneurial endeavor was over before it began. Initially my morning sickness made regular appointments difficult to keep and the smell of nail products unbearable. After Kendall was born, breastfeeding also made any schedule irrelevant. I never admitted to Mark the real reason for abandoning my nail business. In addition to my meager customer base, one day as I was giving a friend's husband a pedicure, it occurred to me, *Washing other people's feet sucks.* No wonder the Pope only did it once a year. There was a reason manicurists have less prestige than estheticians and hair stylists: toes. All other explanations given were just plausible excuses.

Besides, morning sickness aside, pregnancy was an exciting endeavor. Parties were thrown for me, and gifts bestowed upon me. Most people were nicer to me. I bought lots of adorable baby clothes and educational toys. I also bought lots of maternity clothes; even more were given to me. The preparations for the arrival of my first child took all my time. I did not have a clear idea what would happen after his birth, but I assumed caring for him would involve a hefty time commitment. In truth, I had no idea what I was getting myself into. Considering what followed next, that was probably a good thing, but the same thing could probably be said for most parents.

FIFTEEN

....

BIRTH IN THE TIME OF PLAGUE

People were getting sick, some were even dying, and no one knew why. In the weeks leading up to my due date, reports began surfacing out of southern China of a flu-like disease hospitalizing and in some cases killing people. Just as mysteriously, those reports abruptly stopped. In February 2003, I departed Shanghai for Hong Kong to deliver my child. At that time, the *South China Morning Post* picked up the story as cases of catastrophic respiratory distress began to mount. There was still no name for the disease. In the face of the unknown, precautionary measures, effective or not, appeared. Medical masks began spreading across the faces of Hong Kong, and bottles of hand sanitizer were hoarded.

I remained holed up at a townhouse on the south side of Hong Kong Island near Repulse Bay. Mark's boss, who was vacationing in New Zealand, generously lent it to us. I would not recommend spending the last month of pregnancy alone, especially during an epidemic. I may not have had a lot of friends in Shanghai, but I had none in Hong Kong. My contact with the outside world was limited to visits to my obstetrician, Dr. Lam, and grocery runs to Stanley village. Mark managed to visit most weekends, but that left five other days of the week to fill wandering around a home that was not my own and wondering if I was at the epicenter of the next Black Death.

When my due date passed without my baby's arrival, Dr. Lam decided to give him one more week to show up.

"That placenta isn't meant to last forever," the doctor explained.

At the end of the week, with no sign of our baby or even an inkling of his imminent arrival, Mark and I made our way up Victoria Peak. We were able to make the taxi journey at a leisurely pace, rather than hurtling past tour coaches as I had feared. We checked into the Matilda Hospital, which was as serene and luxurious as advertised, despite the ongoing health crisis.

As Mark and I settled in for what I suspected might be our last night of uninterrupted sleep for the rest of our lives, the screaming started, and it was not coming from me. Before long, the decibel level climbed even higher when an additional screamer augmented the primitive cries of the first screamer. Both rooms on either side of mine were now hosting delivering mothers who arrived at the hospital past the point when an epidural could be administered. I did not get any sleep that night. I stared at the ceiling in abject horror, dreading what was in store for me the following day. I looked accusingly at Mark the next morning. He mumbled something about needing a coffee and ducked out of the room.

Shortly after Mark's coffee run, my anesthesiologist arrived. Dr. Yao looked as if he could moonlight as a Brooks Brothers model, not that he needed the money as an anesthesiologist. Stylish in his double-breasted navy blazer and skilled with epidural needle placement, I secretly nicknamed him Dr. Yaoza. Thanks to him, I had one of the best days of my life. That epidural meant I spent the next six hours drinking Diet Coke and munching out while watching old episodes of *Ab Fab*.

In the early afternoon Dr. Lam showed up to check my progress.

A quick peek and he exclaimed, "Oh, wow, you're at nine centimeters. Let me grab a quick lunch before we begin. Be right back."

Dang. I did not want my good time to stop. I definitely did not want the pain to start. Sure enough, they cut me off both the Diet Coke and the epidural in the afternoon in order to push the baby out. When Dr. Lam returned, he looked like a CDC first responder to a plague outbreak. I did not know if Dr. Lam always dressed in what looked like a hazmat suit for deliveries or if I looked especially virulent. I was laughing too hard to feel indignant.

Five weeks after my arrival in Hong Kong, my son was born, a week late and on St. Patrick's Day 2003. Mark and I planned to name him Kendall, and now we added his appropriate middle name, Patrick. The disease also had a name by then, Severe Acute Respiratory Syndrome (SARS) and a global epidemic alert from the World Health Organization. SARS spread to several cities around the world, notably Toronto and Singapore. Thousands of people were infected and hundreds died from the disease, but millions were alive and unaffected, at least physically.

However, a palpable sense of panic gripped Asia, Hong Kong in particular. Despite this, I booked a Cathay flight with Kendall when he was nine days old. I was ready to get out of someone else's house and go home to Shanghai, even if I had to brave a disease to do it. Hong Kong's gorgeous Chek Lap Kok Airport was normally thronged with travelers. However, when I departed with Kendall, it was eerily deserted. For a moment, it looked like a post-apocalyptic world.

SIXTEEN

FOREIGN OBJECTS

The climate and air quality in Shanghai are practically pestilential most of the year, but winter showed Shanghai to an advantage. The normally turbid skies cleared, the odor-laden air dissipated, and the mosquitoes died. On an appealingly brisk December day, I woke Kendall from his nap, and we set out for our weekly playgroup. Although, at nine months, Kendall and his playmates did not actually play together. For most of the afternoon Kendall and the other babies crawled around cramming various objects in their mouths and drooling everywhere.

Among other things at playgroup, I could look forward to an abundance of sage advice offered by child-rearing experts, most with exactly one child each. That particular playgroup was held at the home of Sasha, a koala-cute Aussie with a gorgeous daughter who looked like her name—Amber. Amber had done everything first in our playgroup: first to feed herself, drink from a cup and say "mama." I expected new theories in quantum physics before long thanks to the miraculous Amber. Certainly this indicated what an outstanding mother Sasha was—a natural. Since my little man was the last to do everything, I was the parenting malingerer of the group.

At the time, I was riveted by the plight of the Emperor penguins captured in a popular docu-drama as they tried to perpetuate their species. As a result, I adopted the mantra "keep the egg alive." In a rare burst of confidentiality, a father admitted to me that once the "egg" becomes a teenager, the mantra will change to "don't kill the egg."

With Christmas just a few weeks away, Sasha thoughtfully scattered Christmas ornaments on the floor along with some toys for the kids to play with. Kendall, my egg, put everything in his mouth; a habit he would continue for another nerve-racking year. I assumed his mouthing of objects was a phase he would grow out of, so I did not do much to discourage it. However, failing to examine what he was putting in his mouth proved to be a tragic mistake. Kendall quickly found an ornament and began mauling it.

I was only arm's length away from him when I noticed that he was gagging. I suspected the worst and launched into CPR mode. I vaguely remembered the first step in CPR was to "clear the airway," and I attempted a finger sweep of the mouth. Unfortunately for Kendall, I pushed the foreign object deeper into his throat. Fortunately for me he does not know any good lawyers.

State-Sponsored Sex

I flipped him upside down and began swatting him on the back. He began howling at this betrayal, first the fingers in his mouth and then sharp blows to his back. All I knew was that howls were good—it meant air was getting through. I saw nothing ejected from his mouth. For once I would have been fine with projectile vomiting.

The playgroup crowd stood paralyzed by the spectacle—me more crazed-looking than usual and Kendall crying.

"Did you see anything pop out of his mouth?" I asked Kaori, a micro-Asian woman and mother of three from Japan.

"No, but I'll look," she replied helpfully and got down on her hands and knees and began searching the carpet. "What did it look like?"

"I didn't see it. I only felt something hard just before my finger-sweep shoved it down his throat," I said.

By now a few of the other moms had joined the search for the mystery object. My son's crying had tapered off to a wounded whimper.

"Thanks for looking—but I have to assume he swallowed it. I need to get him to a hospital in case this object tears his esophagus or blocks his intestines. Sasha, can you call me a cab?"

"Just use my driver. He's not doing anything," she offered, in a somewhat cavalier manner, or maybe that was just my imagination.

I rushed out to the minivan in the driveway and climbed in.

"*Wo yao chu port o man*," I instructed the driver in my survival-purposes-only Chinese. The Portman Centre housed the medical clinic we used for routine medical care.

It was late afternoon, and the traffic moved disappointingly, though not surprisingly, slow. Along the way I managed to phone Mark and assure him that yes, his firstborn child was still alive and breathing, but no, the foreign object he was chewing on just before he began choking had not been located. Forty-five agonizing minutes later, I arrived at the clinic to find both my husband and Mr. Chang looking equally distraught. We rushed into the waiting room and were quickly ushered into an examination room. A young, female doctor entered just seconds behind us.

"I understand your child may have swallowed something? What did it look like?"

"Uhh, I think it was part of a Christmas ornament. Actually, I may have pushed it down his throat when I was trying to sweep it out," I explained in a voice I imagined accented with ineptitude.

"Let's put him up on the table and take a look," she said. She retrieved a tongue depressor from a jar and attempted to insert it into Kendall's mouth. He responded with firmly closed lips.

"Sorry, little man, we need to look inside your mouth. Open up, please," I requested, and he parted his lips only slightly, suspiciously. It was enough of an opening for the doctor to slip in and take a quick look. Kendall focused on me with a betrayed look in his eyes; it would not be the last one of the day or, come to think of it, the rest of his life. The doctor then placed her stethoscope on his chest for a quick listen. He squirmed as the cold instrument stung his skin.

"There does not appear to be anything obstructing his airway," she concluded, but so had I, like an hour before. "But you say you could not find the object. That means it could be in his stomach by now. I suggest an X-ray to be certain."

"Okay," Mark and I replied in unison.

"Unfortunately our X-ray machine is down. You will need to go to the foreigners' unit at Rui Jin University," she said, handing us a card with the address.

Our hearts sank. We were not enthusiastic about visiting a local hospital. As most parents quickly discover, once you have children, your relationship with the health care system intensifies. You see more doctors, more often, than you typically do as an adult, and that was just for routine checkups and vaccinations, never mind the inevitable accidents that occur. I knew that, in the event of an accident or sudden illness, I would have to rely on the medical care available in Shanghai. Frankly, I hoped that day would never come. Sure, Shanghai had the world's first Maglev train, an ultra-modern airport and river-spanning bridges and tunnels employing the latest in civil engineering technology. But their hospitals were scary.

Mr. Chang was waiting with the car running. In a city as large and sprawling as Shanghai, he had an incredible ability to find any address in remarkable time. He employed all his professional driver skills, and some insanity, to get us through the heaving and impossibly narrow surface streets on the way to the local hospital.

Mr. Chang pulled up to the front gate and sprang from the car with speed and agility astonishing in a portly smoker. The hospital security guard looked up at Kendall and me and pointed us in the direction of the foreigners' unit. The reception area was confidence-inspiring, with polished floors and uniformed personnel. The Western medical clinic had called ahead to alert them of our impending arrival, so they were expecting us. We were quickly directed to the radiology department.

Once we passed through the doors of the foreigners' unit and into the hallway of the local hospital, dread returned. I know it was cliché to talk about the medicinal smell of hospitals, but that would have been preferable to the odor that confronted us. The tangy stench of urine assaulted our noses immediately as we passed the public toilets. The corridor was brightly lit with fluorescent lighting that showed everything to a disadvantage—the missing tiles from the floor and the dirty, stained walls. Chinese patients and their families milled about and stared at the *weiguoren* walking past them. We arrived at the radiology department and after a short wait were escorted into the X-ray suite. Our confidence returned when we saw the big, beautiful, state-of-the-art Philips X-ray machine. We were pleased to discover that the room temperature, normally frigid in Chinese public buildings during the winter, was kept soothingly warm. Technicians placed protective vests around Mark and me. We were instructed to hold Kendall still as the device moved over him. We did as instructed. He looked so small and vulnerable on the table with no shirt on. He was scared and crying. Mark and I were scared and trying not to cry. I felt as if I had failed him. Had I been more attentive, he may never have swallowed whatever it was making its way through his little body.

We were asked to return to the foreigners' unit to await the results. Shortly thereafter a throng of lab coats appeared and began deliberating. Lots of people wear lab coats and surgical masks in China, so what their occupations were was anyone's guess. Soon a woman who identified herself as the interpreter approached us.

"Unfortunately, the X-ray was inconclusive—we could not locate the object," she rattled off crisply, with only a hint of an accent. "Therefore, the doctors suggest that we put your child under anesthesia and go in and look for the object with a gastric scope."

"Uh, could you excuse us for a moment?" I stammered back, much less articulately.

"Oh-my-God, are they crazy?" I hissed at Mark. "They want to go on a fishing expedition in Kendall's stomach." Before he could answer, I whipped out my mobile and punched in my friend Mary's number. She had caller ID, so she knew it was me.

"Helloooo, whatcha doin?"

"Sorry, no time for chitchat. I am at Rui Jin Hospital, the egg swallowed something, and they are proposing a rather radical solution. Do you have Dr. Leung's number?" Dr. Leung was the pediatrician we had both used in Hong Kong.

Mary rattled off the doctor's number before disconnecting.

I dialed and was astonished when the doctor answered after the second ring. After I explained the situation to him, he paused momentarily before responding.

"Normally, we would wait a few days to see if the object passes before such an aggressive intervention."

I quickly and quietly related to my husband the gist of Dr. Leung's advice that we then relayed to the interpreter. She returned to the throng of lab coats, where there was much intense deliberation. She returned, looking grim.

"If you do not wish to search for the object and instead want to wait for it, the doctors think it best that your son remain in the hospital overnight."

"Thanks...but I think we will be more comfortable at home," I said.

State-Sponsored Sex

The hospital staff was disappointed with our decision but in the end accepted it. We paid our bill and returned home. Kendall seemed fine that evening and slept through the night. The following day he was constipated for the first time that I could remember. The interpreter from Rui Jin Hospital called to check on him. I can never recall a clinic or hospital in the U.S. making a follow-up call. I was grateful but had nothing to report. We continued to wait.

The next morning Kendall had his regularly scheduled morning poo. After attaching a clean diaper, we set him on the floor to play and commenced the grisly task of examining the contents of his diaper. We both donned rubber gloves and began our inspection. I was the first casualty. Overcome by the odor I dropped out. But Mark, God love him, soldiered on. After a few minutes of meticulous scrutiny, he declared the diaper free of any foreign object.

Later that morning, after Mark had gone to work, the egg had a second poo. I knew I had to screw up the courage to go it alone. This time, in addition to the rubber gloves, I added wads of toilet paper up my nose and dove in. Mercifully, my gloved fingers immediately hit something hard and non-biodegradable. There it was—the little plastic piece that connects the ornament with the wire tree hanger. It was not quite an inch long with a circular piece on one end and a dagger-shaped piece on the other. I bundled up the soiled gloves inside the diaper and along with its contents happily dropped it into the Diaper Champ and went off to call Mark with the good news.

"Mark, I found the object. It passed!"

"What did it look like?"

"Scary actually. It was pointed on one end and rounded on the other. We're lucky it didn't do any damage in there."

"What did you do with it?"

"What do you mean, do with it? I threw it away."

"What! Go get it. We have to save that for posterity."

Once again, I dawned gloves and nasal tissue wads, opened up the Diaper Champ, and retrieved the souvenir. *How strange*, I thought as I examined the object after thoroughly washing it in anti-bacterial soap. To think that item passed completely through Kendall's little body.

Later that day the interpreter called again to check on our son and the status of the foreign object in his body. She seemed as relieved as we were when I relayed the good news.

Some day Kendall will also marvel at the object that passed through him. At the time, he was simply content that the constipation had passed. For the moment, I could breathe easier, the egg lived.

SEVENTEEN

TOUGH TITTIES

"Pendulous."

That one-word description of her breasts, written on my mother's medical chart by her obstetrician, made my mother self-conscious about her breasts for the rest of her life.

My breasts did not suffer the same fate as my mother's, but they did not escape ten months of utilitarianism unscathed.

I was her seventh child, and despite the fact that we shared the same gender, I was not comfortable discussing my mom's breasts with her, and now when I looked at her, I had trouble doing so without staring at her chest. She was still complaining about the callous pronouncement made by her obstetrician at a routine checkup many decades earlier. I was unclear as to what was more disturbing to her, the doctor's word choice or the condition of her breasts after the birth of her first child. A condition arrived at despite the fact that my mother, and millions like her, had chosen the bottle over the breast. A choice I wrongly assumed spared breasts from postpartum disfigurement. My mother's childbearing years coincided with the ascendancy of baby formula and the decline in breastfeeding in the mid-twentieth-century America.

Perhaps I harbored a lingering resentment that despite my birth coming a decade after the founding of La Leche League I, like my siblings before me, was raised on formula. We never discussed the toll childbearing took on her body again, but successive inflating and deflating over the fifteen years it took her to have seven children could not have been kind to her belly or her breasts. God only knows what seven births did to her vagina.

I got it. As a mammal, I was equipped for infant nutrition delivery. Those glands had a job to do that did not involve the cover of *Maxim*. In addition to being free, breast milk was reported to result in a higher IQ and a stronger immune system in the baby. Mothers benefitted from an increase in oxytocin receptors and a reduced rate of breast cancer. My obstetrician confided to me that some women even experienced orgasms when they nursed, which coming from someone who looked twelve made me feel like a perv. Not that I was very optimistic, my primary avenues for that function had an unimpressive track record. My G-spot remained undiscovered, and my clitoris, unreliable. The prospect of my nipples succeeding where the varsity team had failed seemed unlikely.

State-Sponsored Sex

Unsurprisingly, I would have to content myself with the promised clinical benefits of breastfeeding. I appreciated that breastfeeding was the right thing to do for my baby, but what I continued to fret over was what it was going to do to my girls. My mother's breasts drooped without dispensing a drop, what would mine look like after several months of hard labor?

I tried to push the aesthetic ramifications of childbearing, not to mention breastfeeding, out of my head. However, in addition to my mother's unsolicited disclosure, I could not shake an unsettling image from my mind. While undressing in a spa changing room, I caught a glimpse of another woman just before she slipped on her robe. All the ravages of childbearing seemed to have settled in her chest. Her naked breasts looked like deflated balloons. Years later the image was still seared on my brain. I assumed that having children had sucked out any abundance that may have once resided in those two little sacks, each capped with what looked like a raisin.

At my baby shower, a veteran mom with four children dismissed my concerns about the physical consequences of pregnancy by assuring me, "Saggy boobs are a small price to pay for the joys of motherhood." I was not convinced, but I was already in my third trimester.

Up until the birth of my son, my breasts had been living a life of leisure, resting comfortably in Victoria's Secret's padded push-up bras—quite literally resting on a shelf. By the third trimester of my pregnancy, however, my breasts were considerably larger than their modest pre-pregnancy B cups, unfortunately they were offset by my even more expansive belly. Once I gave birth, however, the ratio reversed. Indeed, once my milk came in I was ready for breastfeeding and the online porn industry. There were so big they intimidated me. The only drawback was that they were as hard as unripe melons, and they hurt.

A good way to ignore the consequences of pregnancy was to get caught up in preparation for the new baby. A must-have item for any mother-to-be planning on breastfeeding was a breast pump. I received the Medela Pump in Style at my baby shower. It was the finest breast pump on the market, with a powerful motor that allowed simultaneous pumping of both breasts. Pumping for the first time, especially with an electric dual-pump system, I had no idea what to expect. I was afraid it was going to hurt, but it did not, which given the extent to which my breasts were squeezed and pulled was amazing. But I did watch in morbid fascination as my breasts were mechanically sucked to the sound of the whir and whiz from the pump. I was like a dairy cow, without the federal subsidies.

As a mammal, I assumed breastfeeding would be instinctual, for the baby and me. Unfortunately, many things can go wrong with breastfeeding, all exclusively with the mother and involving escalating levels of pain. Nipples become sore, then crack and bleed. Hard bumps

State-Sponsored Sex

from blocked ducts develop in the breasts themselves. Thrush, a yeast infection in the baby's mouth, can be transferred to the mother, resulting in stabbing pain in the breast after nursing. I experienced all of the above during the first few weeks of nursing. I threatened to quit daily. Given how common thrush was, I was dispirited to learn that my doctor lacked medication to treat it in me. Instead, she directed me to dispense the cherry-flavored drops into my son's mouth, and then rub some on my nipples. Now my breasts were big and hard, and my nipples sweet and sticky. I had never felt less sexy or sounded so dirty.

My breasts weren't the only casualties of pregnancy. I breastfed from my mammary glands located on my chest, and yet still developed an udder down below. True, it was only visible when I bent over, but I knew it was there, lurking just beneath my shirt. It may have been a small price to pay for motherhood, but I still was not willing to pay it. I hoped liposuction would solve my bovine problem. A plastic surgeon broke the sad news, "You don't have excess fat; what you've got there is excess skin. Liposuction won't fix that." Well, fuck. Confirming the validity of the wives' tale that misfortune strikes in threes, in addition to the toll my son's voracious appetite took on my breasts and the eventual failure of my abdominal skin's elasticity to accommodate his extended stay in my uterus, my son's ample head imparted an unwelcome gift that keeps giving at inconvenient times. It is called urinary stress incontinence. It has made trampolines and jumping jacks things of the past, and sneezes a thing to be feared.

EIGHTEEN

MARKET DRIVEN

Of the things I wished I had done prior to having children, right up there with laser hair removal and permanent makeup, was something that would alleviate the onerous food-shopping task in Shanghai. Consolidating the task of food shopping sooner would have spared me rock-hard boobs and saved me time with the dual-action breast pump.

Grocery shopping in Shanghai was typically a daylong affair involving multiple stops. The grocer with the best selection of Western products was located in the Puxi neighborhood, a thirty- to forty-five-minute drive from my neighborhood, Pudong. Bakery items involved a trek to Hong Qiao, another thirty minutes out from Puxi, where both the European baker, who sold breads and pastries, and the Mediterranean baker, with more traditional Middle Eastern products like pita bread, bagels and hummus, had their storefronts. Not far from both was a German deli located in a Japanese hotel that sold fish, meat, cheese and a smooth pâté worth the trip alone. That was easily a forty-five-minute diversion, longer if it coincided with lunch and I was forced to stop by the hotel sushi bar. The florist was on Maoming Lu, located in a former dog-racing track. Getting there required navigating a complex web of surface streets. All of this travel was complicated and prolonged by ever-increasing traffic congestion.

The idea to start a farmers' market in my neighborhood came to me about ten months after Kendall was born. Mark and I enjoyed taking morning strolls exploring Shanghai neighborhoods. One morning our stroll took us through a row of bleak, pollution-stained apartment buildings adjacent to our gated community. We came across a mini farmers' market in progress. No one was strolling around with a latte in one hand and a *New York Times* Sunday edition in the other. It was a small gathering of scruffy vendors with meager offerings and contentious senior citizens tight-fisting their *renminbi*. There were two young boys with a flatbed cart attached to their bicycle. A few lonely misshapen vegetables waited expectantly on the cart for interested buyers. Two elderly ladies were examining the goods and initiating negotiations with the boys.

Another vendor was a marvel of engineering modification. Who knew a 50 cc Honda scooter could aspire to be so much more than merely basic transportation? The one I drove in college looked nothing like this. This scooter had transmogrified into a food delivery and production vehicle. The scooter was

State-Sponsored Sex

mostly obscured by its upgrades. Attached to the left rear side of the scooter was a propane tank. Behind it was a large pot with a burner under it. On the right side was a collection of cages, many with live chickens in them. Across the seat were a butcher block and a large knife.

There was a fair amount of blood, feathers and unpleasant-looking globs in the vicinity of the scooter. The vendor smiled pleasantly and nodded as we looked her way. A prospective customer approached her and began looking in the cages, inspecting the flock. Quite a bit of banter was taking place between the chicken vendor and the customer, as well as the incarcerated chickens. Eventually a chicken was selected, and we looked on in morbid anticipation at the fowl carnage to come.

Holding the chicken upside down by its feet, the chicken vendor expertly wrung its neck upward. It gave easily with an audible snap. The chicken's wings flapped uselessly in surprise. As soon as the last spasms of life had left the chicken, the vendor got to work. Expertly, almost artistically, she cut around the anus and worked the intestines and internal organs out. Some of these she tossed on the ground; others she set aside. Now I saw what the hot water was for. Using long tongs, she plunged the chicken into the water. After removing the chicken, she plucked it, placed it in a shopping bag along with the saved organs, and handed it to the waiting customer. Honda engineering meets Chinese ingenuity and service.

I was not looking to recreate the crafts and quilts markets found on weekend mornings across the U.S. What I had in mind was a real market with bread, vegetables, fruit, flowers and wine. True, there was no shortage of markets in Shanghai, as Mark and I discovered in our own backyard. However, I was interested in a market that sold Western-style food for expats.

I convinced the skeptical staff at my neighborhood management office that there was a need for the market. Sensing I was not going to accept rejection, they agreed to let me use the lobby of the clubhouse but remained unenthusiastic. As China transitioned to a modern economy, many Chinese were shopping at the rapidly multiplying chain grocery stores. The management office likely saw open markets with multiple vendors as old-fashioned and unappealing to our neighborhood's urbane population. They may have assumed that most foreigners would be unwilling to shop for food items outside a grocery store. But our neighborhood was international, and the market tradition still thrived in Europe. In the U.S. markets had been seeing a revival. Moreover, Stepford Villas was retro, full of housewives who did most of their shopping during the day on weekdays. I had a sense that I was not the only one who did not care to spend a day in stop-and-go traffic chasing down bagels and baking soda. I also thought I was not the only housewife that wanted fresh ingredients.

Now that I had a venue of sorts, I set out to recruit vendors. I persuaded both bakers to attend. The European baker agreed reluctantly; the Mediterranean baker was more enthusiastic. I soon discovered that the two bakers did not get along. Despite his reluctance, the European baker called the Mediterranean baker shortly after I departed his store and downplayed the market. At the same time he was voicing skepticism for the market, he nonchalantly offered to display some of the Mediterranean baker's wares for him. The Mediterranean baker was suspicious of his rival's motives and related this intrigue to me when I visited him just minutes later to request his attendance. He was enthusiastic until he heard the operating hours. I had decided on Friday mornings from seven until ten, to coincide with the school bus schedule. I thought bakers were used to early hours, but he was a young guy that also wanted to sample Shanghai's boisterous nightlife.

"Sorry," I told him, "the day and time are set. If anything, we might start even earlier."

He grimaced at that comment. He continued to voice his complaint every week, despite the large crowds that began gathering by seven in the morning. I continued to ignore him and purchase my rugelach with a shrug and a smile.

The florist I approached did not have to be convinced. He eagerly agreed. He saw the potential in the market even more than I did and arrived with a truckload of flowers and several assistants for our first market day. Despite what looked like the contents of an entire greenhouse, the florist sold out.

The vendor that I most wanted, and, in fact, did not think I could hold the market without, was the vegetable farmer. I tried to convince Sky Long, farmer Long's wife, to attend the market. She expressed both her and her husband's skepticism. They already had a system in place for delivering vegetables to our neighborhood and did not see a reason to change. After much cajoling and pleading, the Longs reluctantly decided to give the market a try. Because, really, how could I call it a farmers' market without an actual farmer in attendance.

Locating a fruit vendor proved challenging. Eventually I turned to Mark's assistant for advice. She informed me that someone would show up that day with fruit, but did not elaborate further. She was right; two young boys, no more than eleven or twelve years old, arrived on a bicycle with a flatbed attached to the back. It was loaded with fruit. Initially they looked a little nervous, but they quickly lost their jitters and became hard-bargaining salesmen.

The first market included the core vendors offering baked goods, vegetables, fruit, flowers and wine. The European baker was skeptical of the market's ability to attract customers. He only sent a token representative with just two trays of pastries. She quickly sold out everything she brought. When I saw her standing in

State-Sponsored Sex

front of an empty table, she assured me the baker was on his way with more items. He showed up thirty minutes later in a taxi piled high with bread and pastries.

The neighborhood management staff was stunned by the turnout. The clubhouse was thronged with people crowding in front of the various vendor tables, purchasing everything the vendors brought. All of the vendors were ecstatic. Each merchant sold nearly all the products they brought. They all enthusiastically agreed to return the following Friday, and every Friday after that. The European baker admitted that in those three hours he did as much business as his store did all day on Saturdays, his busiest day of the week.

I started to get lots of visitors at my house. People began showing up at my front door with gifts of food and handicrafts, hoping for a place at my market. Anyone selling food that I thought my neighbors would like I gave a spot until we ran out of space. The management company moved the market to a permanently constructed tent in an unused parking lot at one corner of the neighborhood. Customers came from all over Shanghai, with the average crowd around three hundred people. We filled the tent with more than twenty-five regular vendors. In addition to our initial vendors, we added an Italian chef who sold homemade sauces and pastas, an Indonesian chef who sold prepared meals, a fishmonger and a yogurt maker. There was occasionally chaos when a vendor invited a friend to sell products. That was how I ended up with squatters selling eggs. But it was also how I added another popular regular, a couple of German guys selling sausages and smoked meats. Relations between my bakers never improved. To keep the peace I arranged the market layout so that they were on opposite ends. However, I would still catch them glaring at one another from their respective corners. Occasionally words were exchanged, but generally everyone was too busy to get into trouble.

Sky Long came every Friday with a small army of workers. I gave her the largest spot, the entire back wall of the tent. At opening time it was bursting with earth's bounty. By ten o'clock a few stray leaves were often all that remained. Every time I saw her she was smiling, and that was gratifying. Even her husband, Farmer Long himself, came to the market a few times. Originally from Minnesota, Farmer Long took immense pride in his product, explaining to me in detail the pedigree of the seeds he used. The romaine, he assured me, was the same variety grown in California. All of the produce the Longs sold had been picked the day prior. The Longs' carrots tasted sweet, like only home-garden ones could. Sky Long convinced me to try arugula for the first time, pointing out its nutty flavor. It became my favorite salad leaf.

Not only did the market make my grocery shopping faster, but it unwittingly exaggerated my Stepford transformation. Sure, I had been working on my kitchen skills since Mark and I married, but when Kendall came along, cooking was elevated from a pastime to a passion.

State-Sponsored Sex

I was no longer satisfying adult taste buds, I was nurturing new life. At Friday's market I loaded Kendall's wagon with fresh vegetables and, upon returning home, made large batches of baby food from fresh broccoli, carrots and cauliflower. In addition to my daylong cooking project, I filled every room in the house with fresh flowers from the market. At dinner I dressed our mixed-leaf salad from the Longs' farm with house-made Italian dressing from Chef Lino, an Italian chef who also sold fresh pasta and pasta sauces at the market. And breakfast consisted of yogurt delivered in charming glass jars every Friday by a French guy and his Japanese wife.

After a year I turned over supervision of the market to the neighborhood management office. They did most of the logistical work anyway, securing the tent and assigning neighborhood security to direct traffic. For a while I was the neighborhood hero, everyone thanking me and remarking on what a great success the market was. Eventually my involvement in the market was forgotten.

Although I never earned a dime, or renminbi, from the market, I took pride in its success. After abandoning my manicure business once Kendall was born, I needed a reminder that I could still accomplish something unrelated to childcare or housework.

NINETEEN

STRETCH GOAL

With the debut of the neighborhood market a resounding success, I was free to return to obsessing over my physical imperfections, not all the result of pregnancy, but I used that as a comprehensive excuse anyway. More than a year after Kendall's birth and still my girth had yet to completely retract. Lactation was not the magic wand I had hoped to return my body to pre-pregnancy proportions. Despite losing my pregnancy weight and then some, my waist was still indistinguishable from the rest of my torso. Before I attempted surgical intervention with potential complications, I discovered a local studio in Shanghai that offered Yoga Boot Camp three times a week for one month. Boot camp seemed like just the thing I needed to kick my increasingly bovine figure into G.I. Jane shape. The advertisement mentioned the term Bikram. As a yoga novice, that term was unfamiliar to me. I had taken only two yoga classes before in my life.

My first initiation into the ancient practice of yoga took place at my neighborhood Gold's Gym in Northern Virginia just a few years prior. I got the idea from the Wednesday health section of the *Washington Post*. In an article on yoga, all the devotees quoted were seniors. One woman gleefully reported that she had been unable to do the splits until she was fifty, and she was still doing the splits well into her seventies. I was impressed. The splits were something I was unable to manage in junior high, ending a promising cheerleading career before it ever began. It's okay; I enjoyed the debate team, really. Another man cited improved posture and circulation. They looked good, healthy, and their secret was yoga. I was intrigued. I dutifully paid the $39.99-a-month fee to Gold's Gym just to access the evening yoga class.

That particular class was generic, but that worked for me; I was no yoga snob. I was actually unaware that there were different kinds of yoga. I thought yoga was, well, yoga. I dusted off some old aerobics leotards and set out one brisk autumn evening on my yoga journey. I scurried toward the tiny studio at the rear of the gym that was used for everything that did not involve pumping iron, past the bulky men in stained leather lifting-belts and fingerless gloves. The instructor guided the class through various stretches and poses all the while valiantly trying to talk above the grunts and groans emanating from the free-weight room next door.

State-Sponsored Sex

Subsequently relocating to a Leesburg, Virginia, I began searching for my weekly dose of *namaste*. A Kundalini class was advertised at the Ida Lee Recreation Center. A bearded guy who looked like Ben or Jerry was our instructor. He looked yoga-ish; I was optimistic. Then the breathing exercises started, and they did not stop. Turns out, that was what Kundalini was all about. I thought breathing was just inhale, exhale and occasional deep breaths during family arguments. That the instructor resembled an ice cream vendor was likely my first clue that the class was not going to involve perspiration, but I would not have guessed it would focus on various interpretations of respiration.

So the word Bikram meant nothing to me. The first thing I noticed about the Bikram yoga class was that the room was warm and, given that it was in Shanghai, moist. In Bikram yoga, the room was kept at 105°F. Keeping the room warm as the yogis, as practitioners of yoga are called, work through the poses was intended to assist in ridding the body of toxins while enhancing flexibility. I was perspiring just waiting for class to begin. By the end of class I was desiccated from the loss of every drop of fluid in my body.

Y+ Yoga in Shanghai specialized in all forms of yoga. The most they deviated from the yoga path was hosting a visiting Pilates instructor. It was one of the first yoga studios in Shanghai, and arguably the best, and located in an old building on Fuxing Lu in Puxi, with polished wooden floors, intricately carved Chinese-style doors and a reverential atmosphere. An army of ayis carefully placed mats, towels and bottled water in each room prior to class. I was tempted to call my lean and serious instructor sensei; however, by the end of class I wanted to call her Jack Bauer.

Bikram classes were long, ninety minutes, and consisted of a series of twenty-six poses, or *asanas*, each performed twice. De rigueur breathing exercises did occur at the beginning and the end of class, but sandwiched between them and comprising the bulk of the time were standing and floor postures, roughly half of each. I was looking forward to the floor postures after the torment of the standing series. I foolishly thought they would be easier to do because I was no longer standing. However, the intensity had only just begun its slow ratchet up. At least standing postures like eagle pose, as intricate as a Boy Scout knot, and triangle pose, designed to engage even the most obscure abdominal muscles, did not involve amputation. But limb loss was exactly what I was afraid would happen in fixed firm pose. Fixed firm was a floor pose that required sitting in a "W" and then lying back onto the floor so that the feet were parallel with the hips. I whispered down to my feet, "Don't go," as I feared they were about to break off at the ankle.

Vacationing in the U.S., I saw a sign that prominently advertised a studio specializing exclusively in Bikram yoga. Like just about everything in America, it was located in a strip mall, wedged between Dinero Rapido

State-Sponsored Sex

and Mountain Mayhem Biking. Missing my regular yoga sessions, I decided to give the local version a try. It was like a tawdry affair; it meant nothing to me. Gone were the attentive ayis; instead I was now responsible for supplying my own mat, towel and beverage. Instead of polished wooden floors I encountered dingy, industrial carpet glued onto concrete. The gravitas of my micro-thin Shanghai yogi was replaced with an instructor who managed to condense her autobiography into the ninety-minute class time. In addition to leading us through twenty-six poses, she recapped the quitting of her job in California, her parents' subsequent disapproval and her lack of a serious relationship. Namaste and my waist would not be found there.

After Yoga Boot Camp I tried doing yoga on my own. However, attempting Bikram yoga by placing a mat in my closet with a space heater failed to duplicate the ambience of the original Y+ studio. My asanas have suffered. And the splits? They remain an elusive stretch goal.

TWENTY

UP THE YIN YANG

Navigating the Chinese medical system not only improved my pain tolerance, but my ability to withstand withering humiliation. I understood and embraced the importance of a healthy lifestyle. Frankly, I thought I was taking good care of my health. However, my Chinese hospital experiences provided powerful incentive to embrace preventative medicine with renewed vigor.

In addition to the *Fantastic Voyage* of a Christmas ornament through Kendall, I experienced a Chinese-style mammogram. In the best of circumstances, mammograms are uncomfortable. This one, however, involved my breasts compressed to the thickness of crepes and the subsequent discharge of fluid that must have been expired breast milk from twelve months prior. Between the blind-man masseur and the two mammogram technicians, I was not sure if the Chinese had a significantly higher tolerance for pain, or they just enjoyed fucking with Americans.

Initially, my post-pregnancy complications were aesthetic and, while still unresolved, easily disguised with ruched shirts. Subsequently, mysterious abdominal pain led me to a series of doctor's visits all frustratingly similar—each doctor puzzling over the probable cause of my discomfort as they palpated my abdomen. Tests were ordered and proved inconclusive. Eventually, an internist recommended a colonoscopy. Anxious to discover the cause of my distress, I heartily agreed. Boy, was I in for a surprise.

I did not know precisely what a colonoscopy was until I got home and read the pamphlet the doctor had provided. It sounded less like a medical procedure and more like a cruel prank contrived by drunken frat members crossed with the Central Intelligence Agency. I dutifully choked down the beverage provided by the doctor's office that was intended to clear my intestines and spent a gut-wrenching Sunday draining my digestive tract.

Monday morning I presented myself at the Western medical clinic for my procedure. A hospital translator and a driver transported me in a non-emergency hospital van to a local Chinese hospital. The clinics in China that practice standard Western medical care are typically staffed with physicians that have studied in North America, Australia or the UK. Seeing one of these doctors and obtaining a diagnosis was a familiar procedure. Where things depart from familiar territory is, say, when an advanced procedure like drawing blood is necessary. While the rudiments of these procedures are the same, the milieu is, well, foreign.

In a nation not known for the privacy of private citizens, I should not have been too surprised at what I confronted at the local hospital. I arrived at the ward that performed the colonoscopies. It was an assembly line process. Lined up along the wall in the hallway, people waited their turn for the procedure. Inside the room were two beds, one with the person undergoing the procedure, the other for the person coming-to from the sedation. Hospital staff milled about the two beds. I knew this in advance because the door was open and people were standing in the doorway watching as the procedure was performed.

When confronted with an inevitably humiliating situation, and this happens more frequently than I am comfortable admitting, I always reassure myself by saying, "More than a billion people in this country, what are the odds I see any of them ever again." Thus, I changed into my hospital gown and took my place in the plastic chair queue. A foreigner waiting for a colonoscopy must have been a rare sight because I was now drawing more attention than the activity in the procedure room. I tried not to obsess about the inevitable crowd my colonoscopy was bound to attract. I was doing my best to act nonchalant as I pretended to read the book I brought. This gave me time to consider an upside to this ordeal, other than a diagnosis and subsequent treatment of my pain. My intestinal evacuation the day prior had to be good for the loss of at least a pound or two. Not as substantial as full-blown food poisoning, but I only had it coming out one end.

Interrupting my ruminations, my interpreter indicated that it was now my turn. I did my best to ignore the curious onlookers and looked as mission-oriented and focused as one could in a hospital gown. Another difference between hospitals in the U.S. and those in China was the attire of the hospital staff. In the U.S., most nurses and orderlies wear scrubs and ergonomic shoes. The nurse stationed next to the colonoscopy procedure bed wore heels and a flirty dress. An open lab coat was my cue that she was a procedure participant and not an enthusiastic onlooker. The doctor looked a little more familiar, wearing trousers and a golf shirt under his lab coat. No one spoke to me. Good thing because my interpreter had disappeared. I was simply motioned towards the procedure table. Shortly after lying down I was out, and the next thing I knew, I was being shuffled over to the recovery bed. Were the sheets changed between patients, or was this both a shared experience and shared bedding? Since I was anxious to depart and put this whole medical episode behind me, I willed myself awake and moved slower than I would have liked toward the changing room.

Did the colonoscopy reveal the source of my discomfort? No. It was normal. This prompted the gynecologist I saw in Shanghai to recommend a hysterectomy. I might never use my uterus again, but that did not mean I was eager to kick it to the curb. Seeking a second opinion, I scheduled a visit to my Asian Doogie Howser in Hong Kong. Dr. Lam's advanced ultrasound revealed a perfectly healthy uterus. As a result, he enthused that my uterus could accommodate many more pregnancies. I never discovered the cause of the mystery pain. After a few months, it was gone. Sometimes, the body just has to heal itself.

Maybe I should have gone to a Chinese hospital practicing Traditional Chinese Medicine rather than a Chinese hospital practicing Western medicine? What was clear was that my *qi*, or energy, was likely disrupted by too much *yin*, or darkness. And it does not get much darker than a lower intestine. A tube probing around inside my lower intestine with a rapt audience looking on likely contributed to more yin. Next time I have a mystery pain I think I will try meditation and massage first. They may not be the equivalent to antibiotics or even Aspirin, but they were certain to contribute to more *yang*, or lightness, to augment my qi and provide a buffer to the inevitable yin that comes my way.

TWENTY-ONE

THE KIM AND I

Kim Jong-Il and I had some history. I spent a year of my life planning to destroy his country, and hopefully bring about his demise in the process. It was not personal; it was my job description. I was the air force targeting officer in South Korea tasked with mission planning against North Korea's highest value targets in the event of hostilities on the peninsula: refineries, bridges, ports and, of course, command and control facilities. At the end of my one-year assignment I left South Korea and, I thought, the Kim family behind.

Six years later Mr. Chang and I were returning to Pudong from Puxi when we were directed to pull over to the side of the road. All of the traffic in both directions on Dalian Road was stopped to allow a motorcade to pass. When the motorcade whizzed by, a fizzle of discomfort washed over me: something evil passed. Rumors circulated and were later confirmed in the *China Daily*, Kim Jong-Il had visited Shanghai. That had been his motorcade on its way to the Pudong airport. A man I wanted dead had just passed within fifty feet of me. So close. Another six years passed, and Mark and I traveled to Guangzhou to meet our new daughter and experienced another chance encounter with Kim.

When Mark and I decided to have children, we agreed that we would not resort to extraordinary measures to conceive. If I did not get pregnant, we would accept our fate as a childless couple and move on. When I became pregnant with Kendall just a few weeks after making the decision to try to have kids, we assumed we were impressively fertile. We were wrong. We just got lucky. When we started to work on our second addition to the family, we encountered problems. After multiple miscarriages I decided to get off that emotional roller coaster.

That was when Mark and I began to entertain the idea of adoption. Serendipitously, several of our friends in Shanghai had adopted children. These kids came from different places on the globe, but each one was a bright, beautiful child. Since we were in Shanghai, we made tentative inquiries about adopting a child from China.

Adopting a child was a far more onerous task than conceiving one. There are no accidental adoptions. The background checks, sex offender registry checks, interviews, physical exams, credit checks and letters of recommendation made the process as involved as my top-secret security clearance with the military. The process to complete our dossier, the folio with all our required documentation, took several months to complete. Getting it done was my full-time job. I started in late April 2005 and sent it to the China Central Adoption Agency in August. On December 24, 2005, we received our referral, the letter introducing our child to us. Two weeks later we flew to Guangzhou to pick her up. It was a nine-month bureaucratic gestation.

We booked a room for a week at the White Swan Hotel in Guangzhou. At the time, it was the nicest hotel in Guangzhou. In fact, it may have been the only nice hotel in town. The White Swan was swarming with Americans and their new children. The reason for that demographic anomaly was that the U.S. Consulate in Guangzhou was the only consulate in China that processed passports and visas for the adopted children of Americans.

We picked up Brigitte on Monday morning and immediately visited the consulate to drop off her paperwork so the consulate could begin processing her application for a visa and passport. The plan was to return to the hotel and wait until the items were ready for pickup. We were informed that it would be ready Friday at the latest.

Late Tuesday evening the phone in our hotel room rang. Mark was out at a business dinner, and Brigitte was asleep.

"I'm sorry, madam, but you must check out in the morning," I was told when I answered.

"Huh?" The fog began to clear, and indignation set in. "Wait a second. What? Why? My reservation is until Friday."

I received an impassive and unedifying response. "I'm sorry, madam, you must check out in the morning."

I fumed to Mark as soon as he returned from his dinner. He said he would take care of it in the morning. The following morning, the response he was given did not deviate from the one I received. No reason provided for the eviction, just that we had to go. Murmurings from other parents revealed everyone was getting kicked out.

When she was informed of our predicament, our adoption agency representative initially tried to get Brigitte's passport expedited. In the post-9/11 world, that was not going to happen. Then she realized that since we were not departing China, but rather, returning to Shanghai, Brigitte did not need her passport for travel. We could return home and have the passport couriered to us. We opted to do that rather than find another hotel for the remainder of the week.

Upon our return to Shanghai, the *China Daily* once again dispelled the mystery of our abrupt expulsion from the White Swan. Kim Jong-Il had been in Guangzhou to tour factories and receive economic briefings. We were pushed out of the White Swan to make room for Kim and his entourage.

State-Sponsored Sex

Kendall came into the world in the midst of a global epidemic, and Brigitte joined our family during a dictatorial purge.

TWENTY-TWO

NOT WHAT I EXPECTED

"I think my son might be autistic," I said to the pediatrician as he reviewed Kendall's medical chart while I kept Kendall occupied on the exam table. Kendall had just turned two years old.

"Naw, your kid's not autistic," he said after a brief glance in Kendall's direction.

"But he still isn't talking. Not a single word."

"I wouldn't worry about it. I didn't talk until I was three, and look at me, I'm a medical doctor."

Well, you are the expert, I thought and let it go. I suspected something was wrong with Kendall and was begging doctors to diagnose him with anything. This doctor was one of four pediatricians in three different countries who had seen my son and failed to detect his autism. I not only accepted the doctor's assessment, but I was also comforted by it. I wanted to hear that my son was just fine, and the medical community obliged. I was happy to be cast as the hypervigilant mother. I did not mind if there was something wrong with me, so long as there was nothing wrong with Kendall.

After consistently meeting the milestones in the *What to Expect in the First Year* book for his first ten months, Kendall's behavior began to deviate from expectations as his first birthday approached. I noticed that his playgroup friends were saying their first words, pointing and showing items to their parents. Other clues surfaced over the next year, but as novice parents, Mark and I did not know what to look for. Neither of us had significant exposure to young children and, therefore, had no idea what was typical or normal. This lack of experience also contributed to my suspicion that my insufficient parenting skills were to blame for Kendall's diminished progress.

This pediatrician insisted my son's lack of communication was still within the parameters for normal development, but due to my concerns, he referred me to a speech therapist for an evaluation. She diagnosed Kendall with childhood apraxia of speech, a neurological disorder that affects a child's ability to program and plan speech. I had never heard of it before, or since. She suggested weekly therapy sessions and predicted she would have him talking in three months. We pursued this therapy for more than five months to no effect but at the expense of precious time and, of course, money.

Eventually, the speech therapist informed me that there was nothing else she could do for my son and that he would speak when he was ready. She departed and took her diagnosis with her. This coincided with the emergence of a new behavior of Kendall's, rocking. He rocked while lying facedown with his arms straight and his little hands balled into fists underneath him. This prompted another visit to a different pediatrician. This pediatrician admitted he did not know what, if anything, was wrong with Kendall. He did suggest that we have Kendall evaluated by a behavioral psychologist.

The day after Kendall turned three years old, he and I flew from Shanghai to Hong Kong looking for answers. This was the last time Kendall would have no heavier labels than son, boy and toddler. We stayed at the Excelsior, the same hotel where Mark and I stayed on our arrival in Hong Kong six years earlier. We spent a day at the Step Centre of Hong Kong, where Kendall was evaluated by a team of psychologists. The following day we returned to Shanghai, but now Kendall had the diagnosis of Pervasive Developmental Disorder-Not Otherwise Specified, abbreviated as PDD-NOS. Eventually, he would be re-diagnosed with Autism Spectrum Disorder.

Autism was trending, but that did not make it acceptable. Kendall resumed his preschool studies at Dulwich College. Since I was anxious to get started curing him, I scheduled an appointment to discuss his diagnosis with his teacher and the head mistress. I thought as educators they might have ideas and suggestions for early intervention. Also, I was concerned that I would not have him potty-trained by September, a task typically difficult for children with autism, something I learned from one of the numerous websites I had studied trying to educate myself about Kendall's diagnosis. Potty training was not to be taken lightly as it was a requirement for advancement to the next grade at his school. At the meeting, the head mistress did not seem overly concerned. In fact, she blithely remarked that it was only March and helpfully suggested that a lot could happen in the next six months.

A lot did happen, in the next two days. Our meeting took place on Wednesday afternoon. Friday afternoon I received a letter composed on Dulwich College stationery from the head mistress. She wrote to inform me that Kendall's placement in their preschool program was being withdrawn. Her letter explained that because Kendall was not "toilet independent" and would likely not be by September, Dulwich College was "unable to hold a place for him." She did, however, invite me to reapply to Dulwich College should Kendall respond to autism treatment in America. *Not bloody likely*, was my first reaction.

Kendall's options for education in Shanghai were dwindling. Unlike American public schools, international schools were private and could be selective about whom they accepted or rejected. In addition to limited education options, therapy providers were also scarce. I contacted the speech therapist that had unsuccessfully treated Kendall several months earlier for childhood speech apraxia. She informed me via email that her schedule was full, and she was not taking on any new patients. The only other English-speaking speech therapist in Shanghai, she informed me, did not treat children. She also mentioned that she had a "problem" with Kendall's diagnosis. *That makes two of us,* I thought.

I decided to take the advice first offered by the evaluators at the Step Center in Hong Kong and return to the U.S. to get Kendall treatment. The week after I received the letter from Kendall's school and three weeks after his diagnosis, our family flew to Colorado, where we had a vacation condo. The day prior to our departure was Kendall's last day at Dulwich College. His teacher organized a going-away party for him and cried as we said our good-byes. She confessed that the school's treatment of our family had been her worst experience in all her years of teaching. Mark accompanied us to Colorado but returned to Shanghai for work just a few days later.

I naively thought Kendall would get the help he needed in Colorado. However, between the school district and the insurance company, it was like the game of hot potato, both trying to get rid of us as quickly as possible. When I contacted our medical insurer, CIGNA, shortly after our arrival in Colorado, their response was swifter than expected. They informed me that autism was a preexisting condition and not covered by medical insurance. My first thought was, *If it was preexisting, why was I only finding out about it now?* My second thought was, *Bastards!*

Following their evaluation of Kendall, the Eagle County school district in Colorado concurred with the diagnosis he received in Hong Kong. However, it was already May, and the district was reluctant to provide any services during the summer months. They grudgingly offered six hours of speech therapy and six hours of occupational therapy. They never delivered the speech therapy and the occupational therapist was going on vacation, so she combined her sessions into two-hour appointments. The school district's plan for the upcoming school year was to place Kendall into Head Start. Head Start was an early education program designed for economically disadvantaged children, not neurologically challenged ones. The school district was using Head Start as a dragnet for all the young children in the district that had special needs. However, there was nothing in their program that addressed Kendall's autism challenges.

Help did come, however, from unexpected sources. The children's television program *Signing Time* taught Kendall how to communicate using sign language. PBS aired the show on Sunday mornings while we were in Colorado, and after the first show, we each knew more than a dozen signs. Maybe it was time I started pledging. We purchased every DVD in the *Signing Time* inventory. The program started Kendall along the path towards communication. I often invoked Rachel Coleman, the show's creator, because she projected more authority with Kendall than I did. She taught him that knives were sharp, stoves were hot and hands could communicate as effectively as mouths.

In 2006 most autism families were hot potatoes. Insurers denied any coverage, and school districts varied widely in the programs they offered. Which states offered the best education and support for children on the spectrum was a popular topic in online autism forums. Colorado was rarely mentioned.

Even if the school district's offerings were more than meager, it would not have addressed our family's other pressing problem—that we were separated by the Pacific Ocean. It was vital that Mark kept his job in Asia, as we did not need the stress of unemployment compounding the stress of autism on the family. And if we were going to do everything possible to help our son, it was going to cost a lot of money. While I struggled to find help in Colorado, Mark met with the director of a small school in Hong Kong that educated children using Applied Behavioral Analysis (ABA), arguably the most effective treatment for children with autism. Mark convinced his company to relocate the family to Hong Kong while he remained in Shanghai for work. After five months in Colorado, the children and I headed to Hong Kong. What we did not know then was that we would not live together as a family for the next three years.

TWENTY-THREE

SWEET NOTHINGS

After six years of sitting in the back seat of the car and staring at Mr. Chang's head, I was ready to reclaim the driver's seat, even if it meant driving on the wrong side of the road. Mark bought me a ten-year-old Mercedes ML 320, a mid-size SUV, which on Hong Kong roads might as well have been a tank. As a result of a steady diet of *The Wiggles*, the kids dubbed our new vehicle the Big Green Car. In the car park at our apartment, brimming with status cars such as Porsches, Ferraris and Mercedes, we were barely keeping up appearances.

Shortly after getting the car, I decided to embark on a mission. It was both a driving and eating adventure. Somewhere in Causeway Bay, Hong Kong, there was a Krispy Kreme donut shop, and I was determined to find it. None of us had ever eaten an infamous Krispy Kreme donut before. I strapped the kids into their car seats, and we set out in the Big Green Car to find junk-food nirvana. It was not just the sugar rush I craved, but an injection of Americana residing within the depths of Hong Kong.

I was unprepared for Hong Kong traffic. I had no idea what I was getting myself into driving to Causeway Bay on a weekday night at rush hour. Causeway Bay was one of the most densely populated places on the planet. I never did it again. During evening rush hour, the cars snaked down the streets and moved in erratic lurches. The sidewalks were thronged with commuters and shoppers. The din of honking horns accompanied the song "Magic," by one-hit-wonder Pilot, on our car stereo. We slowly wove our way down narrow streets and finally found the brightly lit storefront on Lee Yuen Shan Road, more than an hour after leaving our apartment. I parked illegally across the street, a habit the Hong Kong Police Department would quickly cure me of.

We had come this far, I was determined to return home with the spoils of victory. Even though it was just the three of us, and Brigitte still lacked most of her teeth, I ordered a dozen assorted donuts so we could sample all that Krispy Kreme had to offer. The kids and I made our way back to the Big Green Car for the journey home. Whatever traffic situation we encountered, we were prepared with plentiful rations. I handed each kid a donut and grabbed one for myself. They consumed their first donut with remarkable speed and demanded more. By the time we returned to the apartment, Brigitte was out cold; a sprinkling of powdered sugar ringed her tiny mouth.

We never went back to Krispy Kreme, but I was still disappointed to learn of its demise. Two years after opening, Krispy Kreme Hong Kong closed its doors forever. It was not consumer dietary conscientiousness that killed it, but Hong Kong's brutal retail rental environment. Selling donuts did not pay, not enough to rent in Causeway Bay.

The problem with optimism was that the line between it and naiveté was not clearly delineated. Like the proprietors of Krispy Kreme, we also arrived in Hong Kong betting on success. Arriving in Hong Kong in 2000, I was on an adventure, but returning to Hong Kong in 2006, I was on a mission. I arrived with Kendall and Brigitte, and my plan was to heal Kendall. It was a time-sensitive plan. Autism intervention was most effective the earlier it began. Up to age five the brain undergoes tremendous development. In getting Kendall help, I felt I was racing against the clock. Treating Kendall consumed my time and energy, which left little of either for anything else. Kendall had one-on-one instruction for six hours a day, five days a week. He was the hardest working three-year-old I knew.

Because Mark was gone throughout the week, it was also the beginning of a separate existence for Mark and me. Mark arrived worn out late on Friday evenings. The family spent the next day and a half together; then Mark would prepare for his return journey to Shanghai mid-

Sunday afternoon. I could not shake the irritating reminder that this grand family experiment was his idea. And while I knew in my head that he had to stay in Shanghai for work, my heart was crushed by shouldering the responsibility of caring for our children on my own. I felt like a single parent. Mark felt like a serial houseguest, and we were both exhausted.

TWENTY-FOUR

WASTE MANAGEMENT

Potty training was a formidable challenge. Kendall's continued use of disposable diapers weighed on my environmental soul. In addition to a landfill somewhere with our family name on it, I knew I was merely postponing the inevitable. Although Kendall seemed blissfully unaware of his bodily functions, if he got much bigger, I would have to start shopping for Depends instead of Pampers. Unfortunately, I was more than aware of his bodily functions; I was intimately involved in his digestive process from start to finish. Because his new school prioritized toilet independence, they urged me to begin the task of potty training him, with their guidance. It would take a year to complete. Urine was not the challenge, feces were.

Kendall already accepted that the toilet was the appropriate location for depositing his pee. He did not even wear overnight diapers once he made that connection. It was controlling his little sphincter that was proving to be the challenge for him. There was not a room in our Hong Kong apartment that was not eventually christened with Kendall's poo. He would shuffle around the apartment in search of me, pants around his knees, a trail of poo in his wake. Sitting on the toilet often did not trigger the urge to go; unfortunately, submersion in warm water frequently did.

The bathroom was warm and steamy from Brigitte's bath. Dressed in her pajamas and her hair still wet, she clutched her blanket and watched a *Baby Einstein* DVD while I prepared Kendall's bath. Routine was important to him, so I maintained the same schedule every evening: dinner, playtime, bath time and bedtime. Somewhere in there he usually went poo. That night there had been no poo, so I knew I would have to be vigilant. Something about lying in the warm tub seemed to loosen his bowels. If I was not attentive, he defecated in the tub, which did not bother him, but did distress me.

"Now, Kendall, do you need to go poo?" I asked as I rubbed a handful of Johnson's baby shampoo into his hair.

"No."

"Is it okay to go poo in the tub?" I asked as I rinsed him off, the bubbles dancing down his back.

"No." He sang the word no, drawing it out. He seemed so emphatic that I wanted to believe him.

"What do you do if you need to go poo?" I stood up and replaced the shower head, giving him a stern look as I did so.

State-Sponsored Sex

"Go in the toilet." He had his answers down pat. But his behavior did not always match his intentions.

"Okay, I'll be right back."

That night we had salmon for dinner, which meant more time in the kitchen—the grill pan required scrubbing, and grease splatters extended in a wide radius around the stovetop from the oil in the fish. I realized that I was taking too long, but I was anxious to finish so that the kitchen was cleaned before I got the children into bed.

Once the kitchen was clean, I returned to the bathroom to find Kendall stretched the entire length of the tub, unaware that anything was wrong. He was lying in his own excrement in water a cloudy yellow-brown. Pieces of shit were visible in the water around him. Disgust was too nuanced an emotion for him.

"Kendall! Get up. Wait. No, don't get out of the tub. Just stand there."

"Kendall, did you go poo in the tub?" I asked the obvious question.

"No," he replied, despite ample evidence to the contrary.

"Just stand there. Don't move," I instructed him as I let the soiled water out of the tub and scooped out what I could with soggy pieces of toilet paper.

In what was an unfortunately familiar practice, I rushed to the laundry room and retrieved the large jug of bleach and bathroom disinfectant.

Returning to the bathroom, I found Kendall exactly where I left him, wet and shivering in the tub. I yelled at him anyway.

"Kendall, look what you've done; you've gone poo in the tub," I said as I lathered him with soap again from head to toe.

"No," he maddeningly replied.

"Yes, you did," I screamed, hosing him off. I wrapped a towel around him and carried him to his room. "Put your pajamas on," I instructed, setting him down, and returned to disinfect the bathroom.

My routine began by liberally dousing the area with bleach and then following up with a coating of bathroom disinfectant. Also routine, my fuming. It was bad enough that Kendall went poo in the tub, I seethed, but what was worse was that it did not bother him when he did.

Not all of Kendall's difficulty in proper poo disposal was a lack of awareness or sphincter control. I later discovered that a significant part of Kendall's problem was diet. Testing revealed intolerance to a long list of foods. After I removed dairy and wheat from his diet, he gained control of his sphincter and poo-in-the-tub incidents became rare and then disappeared entirely. Before accomplishing this feat, he did close two public swimming pools. The first time this happened, I noticed that he was walking funny when he emerged from the water, and I grew concerned. When I checked his swim trunks, my suspicions were confirmed; his trunks were full of poo. I alerted the lifeguards and then skulked out

State-Sponsored Sex

of the pool area with Kendall in tow. The second time it happened, he was at the community pool during summer camp. One of the other campers noticed a turd floating in the pool in Kendall's vicinity. His pants were checked, and he was found culpable. The following day another camper had an accident at the same pool. The head counselor told me this, I guess to make me feel better, which it did.

"Mommy, would you read us a story?" Brigitte asked after I disinfected the bathroom and insured it no longer posed an E. coli threat.

"No, Brigitte, it's too late," I said and turned out the light.

First, I needed to take a long shower, and then I needed to pour myself an ample glass of wine. What I could not deal with anymore that night were children. Shared experiences, once a rare luxury I craved with Mark, were now a rare necessity. I was struggling to cope on my own.

TWENTY-FIVE

....

RELIGIOUSLY INCORRECT

I was an unrepentant Archie Bunker. But just like Archie, I eventually got my comeuppance. By the time I relocated to Hong Kong, I had lived in several overseas locations, first with the air force and later with Mark. Despite exposure to different races, religions and cultures, my stereotypes were burgeoning into full-blown bigotry. With 9/11 still a fresh memory, I lowered the bar on my own level of religious intolerance. With the "War on Terror" raging, I did not want to take any chances with people who would like me better dead. Admittedly, that category was not exclusively Al Qaeda; my prickly disposition frequently engendered hostility and burnt bridges. However, because I did not want my demise to be someone else's ticket to martyrdom, I felt justified harboring religious prejudices.

Even though I was not much of a Catholic, when I arrived in Hong Kong, I planned to hire a housekeeper from the Philippines, whom I expected to be a Catholic, good, bad or otherwise. Thus, when I hired Coly, I did not ask her what her religion was because I thought it was a foregone conclusion. My politically incorrect plan backfired when my Filipina helper turned out to be not Catholic, but Jehovah's Witness. She may not have wanted to kill me, but I was as good as dead to her anyway. Since Jehovah's Witnesses believe Armageddon was just around the corner, and they were the only ones going to Heaven, I would soon be dead and in hell—right where I belonged. Considering what came next, that was a fair reckoning.

It was only a matter of time. The apartment across the elevator lobby from ours was empty when we moved into the newly built Bel-Air towers, and remained that way for months. However, new neighbors eventually arrived. I smelled their aromatic food, and it made me feel both ravenous and inadequate. I have not been so motivated to join someone else's family since my childhood spent in the company of savage brothers. The scent of exotic, mouthwatering Indian food taunted me in my own kitchen. I did not have a preference for the nationality of my new neighbors, but I do remember thinking, *Indians are cool; at least they are not Muslims*, somehow forgetting that there was such a thing as Muslim Indians. The Indian neighbors had moved in, and every day I had to fight the urge to turn right towards their door when I got off the elevator instead of left towards mine. I only had myself to blame if their food smelled so much more enticing than mine, but I

State-Sponsored Sex

was no match for their army of Sri Lankan domestic servants.

When I finally met my new neighbors, Khozu and Farida, I casually mentioned how wonderful their food always smelled and was immediately invited to their home for a dinner party. As it turned out, the occasion was not an intimate, seated dinner but a crowded, raucous affair with more than fifty guests. They were new in Hong Kong and already knew that many people? I had been in Hong Kong a year and could count my acquaintances on one hand.

Khozu was the outgoing member of the couple, Farida polite but reserved. Khozu greeted me upon my arrival and immediately offered me a glass of red wine and began introducing me to the other guests. I pointed to a set of photos on the wall of two elderly gentlemen in native garb and asked Khozu if those were ancestors of his, explaining that I was a genealogy nerd. He replied no, those were the imams from their mosque back in New Delhi. At that point, another guest feigned embarrassment about swilling wine in front of the imams' photos and moved off. Indian Muslims. Boy, did I feel dumb. Little did I know, but I looked even dumber.

The universe does not like me, and I cannot really blame it. Apparently, a simple revelation about tolerance and judgment was not sufficient. The powers-that-be determined that I deserved a punishment. Later in the evening, I caught a glimpse of myself in a mirror and discovered to my utter mortification that the hem of my dress was tucked into the waistband of my stockings, affording everyone I passed an unfortunate view of my ass—how apropos. Karma, it turned out, was not only a bitch, but also nondenominational.

Coly told me many months later that Khozu and Farida's son, Hussein, often went out of his way at the playground to greet and engage in play with Kendall. At that time, Kendall's social and communication abilities were nonexistent, so it was unlikely that he reciprocated Hussein's friendly overtures. Most of the other children in our Hong Kong neighborhood openly shunned Kendall, and several called him names. Not that Kendall cared, but it bothered me. I might have deserved that treatment, but Kendall did not.

TWENTY-SIX

SMUGGLER'S POOS

My decision to intentionally infect Kendall with intestinal worms was not the wackiest thing I have ever done to him. Nor was it some misguided attempt to toughen him up. Rather, the intention was to give his immune system something to do other than cause inflammation in his body. Therefore, I introduced parasites into his digestive system. There was even a name for this, helminthic therapy. Admittedly, it was not a fact-based decision, but it was an interesting theory-based decision. The theory was that many maladies experiencing a surge in diagnosis, like Crohn's disease, ulcerative colitis and autism, had an autoimmune component. Something in the environment was causing the body of those with these disorders to attack itself. The theory hypothesized that the trigger for this attack was our now too-clean world, devoid of all the pesky bugs, worms and parasites that plagued our ancestors. However, it was a world our immune system had evolved to survive in over thousands of years. Like me,

Kendall's immune system was looking for meaningful work. In the absence of gainful employment, it was wreaking havoc in his little body.

I imported pig whipworms from Germany. Although, import was not the most accurate characterization for what I was doing; smuggle would be more precise. Most countries work to keep parasites from crossing over their borders. I suspected the Hong Kong Health Department would have objected to my alternative medical therapy, so I chose not to inform them. The worms were sent first to a middleman in Thailand. From there they were sent on to my home in Hong Kong. FedEx was my unwitting accomplice in this escapade. Over the course of several months, my packages of contraband parasites were never intercepted by Hong Kong Customs. Perhaps that department lacked the fervor and zeal of the Parking Enforcement Division of the Hong Kong Police Department, the branch of government I was most familiar with.

As the name implies, pig whipworms were supposed to reside in the intestinal tract of pigs. Since humans were not their natural hosts, they die off after about two weeks, hence the need for recurring doses. When the first shipment arrived, I reverently placed the four little jars of cloudy fluid on the top shelf of my refrigerator. They occupied the same cool real estate as Kendall's other alternative therapies like cod liver oil and B-12 syringes. I said a silent prayer that neither my housekeeper nor I would clumsily knock one of the

State-Sponsored Sex

precious jars to the floor, shattering the glass and spilling its colony of worms onto the cold marble. I did not tell my housekeeper what was in the jars, only that they were medicine for Kendall. I did not need both Customs and Hong Kong's equivalent of child protective services on my ass.

I was anxious to administer the first dose and see what happened. I mixed it with some juice. I did not taste it, a big regret of mine. What was the worst that could happen? God forbid I lose a little weight. I administered and waited. After the initial four dosages, I increased the worm load with subsequent exposures and waited some more. Months of bimonthly worm cocktails and nothing happened, at least nothing that I could see. Fortunately Kendall's poo did not try to wriggle out of the toilet. But neither did his behavior or communication ability change in any discernible way.

I abandoned the effort after several months. Those sanitary worms were expensive little bastards. And while it may have been cheaper and more expeditious if I had simply traveled with my son to a third-world slum and had him eat street food and drink the tap water for a few days, I would have never been sure of the pedigree of the parasites he was ingesting. These worms were the product of German engineering. I was expecting precision and performance—BMW parasites. Instead I paid first-world prices for a third-world experience; money changed hands without a lot to show for it.

TWENTY-SEVEN

UP TO AND INCLUDING VOODOO

I tried not to take it personally, but Kendall's first word was "chip," as in potato. Making matters worse, Brigitte's first word, spoken six months earlier, was "bubbles." And "Mama"? I do not think it cracked the top ten for either kid. I can see my future, and it involves being set adrift on an ice floe.

Now that Kendall was speaking, I expected new words to be added to his vocabulary at a rapid pace. That was the way it was supposed to work. What it took me a while to internalize was that once Kendall's autism was diagnosed, nothing would ever happen the way it was "supposed to." I learned that saying words was not the same thing as communicating. Kendall increased his vocabulary, but teaching him to communicate was an ongoing project. Meanwhile, Brigitte talked enough for the both of them.

Once we arrived in Hong Kong and placed Kendall in the ABA program, I assumed he would be cured in just a few short years. I did not try everything as I had originally vowed because I thought ABA was the cure. A year after our arrival in Hong Kong, during which time Kendall participated in an intensive ABA program, he showed some improvement. Unfortunately, his little school imploded from the strain of a personality conflict between the school's founder and its program director.

We were relieved to find Autism Partnership, a Hong Kong school that used ABA principles but adapted them to a more natural classroom setting. In order to determine the appropriate school placement and therapy approach, however, they wanted to test him again. This time, Autism Partnership gave Kendall the unambiguous diagnosis of Autism Spectrum Disorder (ASD). But more distressingly, I was told that his IQ, about seventy, meant he was intellectually disabled, what used to be called mental retardation. It was the worst thing anyone has ever said to me about my son. Even worse than the mean little girl in our Shanghai neighborhood who remarked when he was just a few months old, "That's not a very pretty baby." I knew both assessments were not correct.

I knew Kendall had talents, and I was hopeful we would discover them together. Even before his diagnosis, while still in preschool he learned his shapes and colors well before his classmates. He had a tremendous memory. When I bought him a puzzle of alphabet letters, I discovered that he could spell at age three. More importantly, he not only spelled simple, three-letter words like cow and pig. When I incorrectly spelled the word rhinoceros with a "u-s" instead of an "o-s," he corrected me. I crashed and burned in the first round of two spelling bees before conceding that spelling would not be one of my core competencies. Good thing I was born in the age of spell check.

I wanted to continue to pursue ABA therapy for Kendall, but now I wanted to augment it with alternative therapies. I found Dr. Tim Trod, a Hong Kong general practitioner willing to try many of the new approaches as long as they were guided by sound theories and Kendall was tested to determine that his health was not negatively impacted.

We began working our way through many of the popular alternative therapies. We removed wheat and dairy from Kendall's diet when the comprehensive blood test conducted by Dr. Trod revealed that while he was not allergic to those foods, he was intolerant to them. In fact, Kendall was intolerant to a staggering number of foods. When Dr. Trod presented me with the test results, and my face fell and my shoulders sagged at the sight of the long list, he reassured me by suggesting that I focus primarily on wheat and dairy. Once we adopted the gluten-free, casein-free diet (GFCF) the eczema that had plagued Kendall since he was a baby finally disappeared. Even more significantly, his stools were no longer loose. For the first time in his life Kendall's feces were consistently firm and formed. This meant greater control and fewer accidents, especially in the bathtub.

Discovered earlier, this insight could have saved a lot of bleach and grief.

Every new therapy required additional testing, usually blood or urine. And virtually every test was positive, which meant something was wrong. Each positive test revealed another problem that required fixing. Toxic metal tests indicated Kendall exceeded the reference range for levels of lead, mercury and arsenic. To address this Kendall took Meso-2,3-dimercaptosuccinic acid (DMSA) for the removal, or chelation, of toxic metals. This was delivered via suppository, not an anatomical location on Kendall I wanted to mess with now that it was operating efficiently, but arsenic sounded serious. Kendall took the antifungal Diflucan to reduce the level of yeast in his body. I gave him injections of methylcobalamine, a form of B-12, every third day to address inflammation in his brain. In turn, he would make my heart ache when he would tell me, "No shot tonight, Mommy." When Vitamin D deficiency became the rage, we had him tested although it was a fait accompli. Of course his vitamin D levels were low. For the most part, the alternative treatments employed consisted of supplements and vitamins. Probiotics such as Mutaflor and *Saccharomyces boulardii* to discourage the growth of pathogenic bacteria and yeast in his digestive tract, cod liver oil to improve cognitive function and Epsom salt baths to detoxify.

Beyond pills and shots, Kendall and I pushed the boundaries of alternative and ventured across the border into just plain wacky. We tried a movement therapy that involved Kendall stepping, crawling and hopping through hoops. Kendall gamely went along. I wanted to tell the practitioner that he was a little boy with autism, not a pedigree canine preparing for the dog show circuit.

I enrolled Kendall in Hippo therapy, which was really just horseback riding. Kendall attended group sessions with other autistic boys who obediently mounted their steeds and rode them in circles for forty-five minutes each week. These were mean, old hags that nipped and butted their handlers but were surprisingly gentle with the children participating in the therapy. After a few months, however, Kendall grew as bored as the horses and no longer attended without protest. He looked so cute in his jodhpurs and riding boots that I hated to quit.

A neighbor recommended NAET. She admitted it sounded crazy, but insisted it had worked for her. NAET was developed by Dr. Devi Nambudripad. Its intended use was the elimination of allergies. According to the advertising literature, it was founded on the holistic principles of oriental medicine, acupuncture, applied kinesiology and allopathy. The Yuen Method blended Chinese Shaolin healing methods and Western science. It was advertised as a powerful, noninvasive healing and empowerment technique. Kendall and I met with a very nice, earnest young woman who confidently assured us the combination of these methods would eliminate Kendall's food intolerances and improve his behavior and communication. She explained that it was all about channeling energy, which she was trained to do. This was a mega mash-up of Eastern and Western healing. Kendall held vials of suspected allergens in the palms of his hands in order to detect sensitivities. The NAET/Yuen Method practitioner placed her hands on Kendall's back and channeled positive energy into Kendall and eliminated the bad energy currently inside of him. Issues of yin and yang had bedeviled me in the past, so I did not immediately dismiss this. Watching her rearrange Kendall's energy looked like a kind of Oriental exorcism, but I decided to let it play out. I am not sure what strained credulity more, the therapy or that I took Kendall to more than one appointment.

Eventually, I found my way to neurofeedback. Neurofeedback uses brain imaging to illustrate brain activity. Children with autism have overactive or overstimulated brain regions as well as inactive brain regions. As a result, parts of the brain do not communicate properly with other parts of the brain. These active and inactive regions can be visualized on a brain map. The practitioner displays the map and helps the child learn how to slow down or speed up their brain waves. The child was rewarded for their efforts with pleasant images and sounds.

Several small studies using neurofeedback showed promise in treating children with autism. However, I could not find a practitioner in Hong Kong. When I contacted a neurofeedback practice in Colorado, they passed my question on to Hershel Toomin, one of the founding fathers of neurofeedback in America. He recommended Dr. Paul Kwong in Hong Kong.

Dr. Kwong was more an enthusiast than a practitioner. Dr. Kwong, who insisted I call him Dr. Kwong, was a retired professor with an interest in neurofeedback. He agreed to treat Kendall at his home. Eager to get started and hopefully see some results, we agreed on three days a week. This came at the expense of his one-on-one ABA therapy. For several months Kendall and I slogged through Hong Kong rush-hour traffic to catch the Discovery Bay ferry in Central Hong Kong. The combined commuting and therapy time added up to a part-time job, more than twenty hours a week.

Dr. Kwong owned a pRoshi device. The pRoshi differs from traditional neurofeedback in that no brain images were visualized. Instead, calibrated flickering lights were viewed through specially designed glasses. According to the pRoshi website, the effect of observing these flickering lights cause the brain to attain "a meditative state in which it becomes totally at rest...yet attentive at the same time—similar to the brain of a Zen Master." No visual images were required because the brain performed its own neurofeedback duties.

For the pRoshi to work effectively, special glasses had to be worn, ideally for thirty minutes or more. Kendall never kept the glasses on for more than three minutes. Dr. Kwong checked with the creator of the device, Chuck

Davis, who believed Kendall would still derive benefit using the device in a darkened room. Kendall began insisting on sleeping with the pRoshi on in his room. At first we turned it off after he fell asleep. Most mornings, however, when we went in to wake him we found the device turned back on. We decided to purchase our own. The pRoshi device cost $2000. Kendall still sleeps with it on every night. It was a very expensive night-light.

After we purchased our pRoshi, we rented a hyperbaric chamber. The rental fee for the chamber was $1000 for the month. To purchase a new chamber would have run approximately $20,000 with shipping. Hyperbaric oxygen therapy (HBOT) increases oxygen to a level higher than atmospheric pressure. The point of this therapy was to increase the amount of oxygen in Kendall's brain and subsequently reduce the level of inflammation. Several small studies indicated it might be beneficial for children with autism. Like most of the alternative therapies for autism, however, mainstream doctors were skeptical.

For the first week either Mark or I climbed into the chamber with Kendall for the dive. After we were confident that Kendall could handle the dives on his own, we put him in the chamber with a portable DVD player, books and toys. I was surprised how compliant he was. The oxygen and pressure were manually operated and required monitoring throughout the dive. Also, once a dive began, the chamber could not be opened until it was returned to sea-level pressure. We learned the hard way to restrict liquid consumption prior or the bladder was emptied in the chamber instead of the toilet.

We rented the chamber twice. During that time, we did notice that Kendall talked more, and his behavior improved. However, he still received daily ABA therapy, and at that time they were focusing on tantrum reduction. The fact that I was often trying several therapies at any given time made it hard to determine what was causing Kendall's improvement.

Kendall made slow and steady progress. For him, there was no breakthrough treatment that reversed his condition. Other parents with children on the spectrum told me they considered Kendall a success story. The daily struggle with a child on the autism spectrum sometimes made it difficult to see improvement. Kendall was better, but he was still autistic.

TWENTY-EIGHT

DICKENS LIVES

Queen Victoria's memory lives on in Hong Kong. It became a crown colony during her long reign. In Hong Kong's Causeway Bay neighborhood, a large park bears Victoria's name and was home to her statue. Also, Hong Kong Island's tallest peak was named for her. However, it was another nineteenth century Brit whose memory surfaced unexpectedly during my time in Hong Kong—Charles Dickens.

I found a contact phone number for the Hong Kong Post Office online and called, expecting a long slog through successive electronic menu messages. Instead, I got a human. On the second ring. Who answered in English.

When we moved into the Bel-Air apartments on Hong Kong's south side, we were provided with our mailing address, which Mark and I efficiently distributed to friends and family, perhaps too efficiently. At the time, it was the correct address. A few weeks after we moved in, however, both our street name and our street number were changed. We were informed after the fact. Although we notified everyone of the new, new address, not everyone updated their address books, especially the luddites still using address books.

When she had not received my acknowledgment of the card she sent for my birthday, my sister emailed to confirm that it had arrived. Because it contained a gift certificate, she was somewhat distraught to learn she had used the old, no longer valid address. I assured my sister that I would track down her card. In reality, I was not optimistic, but I did not share that detail with her.

I explained the confusion with the change of both the street name and number to the competent woman who answered the phone at the Hong Kong Post Office.

"Oh, then you need to contact the Dead Letter Office. Let me give you that number."

Dead Letter Office. Oh. My. God. This was the best.

It sounded so Dickensian. I was intrigued and excited as I made the call. I was not even interested in locating the missing letter anymore. I just wanted to talk to someone from that office. I wondered if I could get a job there.

"Dead Letter Office."

When I heard that, I wanted to squeal with delight. Instead, I explained my problem to the human being who answered the phone, again in English.

"What is your family name?"

"Noble."

"Yes, I have your letter right here." Are you kidding me? In a city of seven million inhabitants, she had my letter right there?

"Would you like to pick it up, or should I have it sent to your residence?"

"Uh, would you send it to me?" I asked timidly, as I felt I had already been an imposition.

"Very well. I will post it tomorrow."

My next surprise came the following morning. I expected the errant letter to arrive with the daily mail delivery. Instead, the letter arrived by courier the following morning. These people were good, very good.

Three years later Dickens' legacy reemerged. In the autumn of 2009 Brigitte was not feeling well. Her symptoms were an odd assortment I had not encountered in little kid illnesses before. Initially, she had a fever and what I thought was the beginning of a cold. When these symptoms abated, I sent her on to school, only to be contacted by the school nurse about a new symptom that had emerged—a red rash on Brigitte's chest. Now that things were getting weird, I made an appointment to see Dr. Trod and was told to bring Brigitte in later that same day.

Brigitte claimed to feel okay, but now she looked flushed as we waited in Dr. Trod's waiting room. I saw Dr. Trod emerge from his exam room and pick up the next medical record in the queue. He glanced at the record and then looked up and called Brigitte's name.

Brigitte and I stood and began to make our way across the waiting room towards the doctor when he exclaimed, "My God, she's got scarlet fever!"

"I didn't know scarlet fever still existed," I said as we sat down in Dr. Trod's office. I had only read about the disease in novels set in the nineteenth century. I assumed it had gone the way of leprosy and fainting couches.

"I know, it sounds so Dickensian, doesn't it?" Dr. Trod enthused.

"How serious is this?" I asked, because the characters who contracted it always died.

"Oh, it's quite mild these days. But it used to be a death sentence." Dr. Trod was clearly craving something out of the ordinary, and Brigitte's anachronistic disease fit the bill.

"Antibiotics for the next five days, and then she can return to school," he instructed. "Also, because this is an infectious disease, you should report it to her school."

While we waited for Brigitte's prescription to be filled, I contacted the school nurse and let her know Brigitte's diagnosis and course of treatment. As we descended in the elevator towards the parking garage located in the basement, my mobile phone rang. On the line was a representative from the Hong Kong Department of Health. I answered her questions about Brigitte's illness and the doctor's treatment. But I was very nervous. Because even though Hong Kong no longer maintained vestiges of Dickens' days like debtors' prisons and child labor, it did quarantine people in its holiday parks in the event of disease outbreaks. Holiday parks were Hong Kong's version of a KOA campground. In the event of quarantine I knew Brigitte would not be going alone. We would both be shipped off to some remote New Territories location. We did not even own sleeping bags. Fortunately, Brigitte recovered at home, and neither of us was subjected to a *Bleak House* experience.

TWENTY-NINE

OH NO HE DIDN'T

Fortunately for our family, Buddhists were an understanding lot. Many Hong Kong business owners were Buddhists who reserved a place in their stores, offices or restaurants for a shrine. Those shrines were not inconspicuous. They typically contained a statue, offerings and lit candles, all with a predominantly red motif. To Kendall, who had no real understanding of religion, those shrines looked like party decorations. Kendall often noticed a shrine before I did and immediately pounced on it, extinguishing the candles. Kendall thought he was blowing out birthday candles, not Buddha candles.

This was one of many reasons that, out of necessity, Mark and I were helicopter parents. Something as straightforward as being seated in a restaurant was fraught with peril. Even before reaching the table and dousing the romantic candlelight, Kendall caused trouble. More than once we arrived at our table in a restaurant only to discover that Kendall already had food in his mouth. It was not difficult to spot where the food came from, the table of angry people staring after us. Even though Kendall was obviously guilty, he exhibited no remorse, only a French fry or potato chip clutched in his fist or protruding from his lips.

The close confines of elevators proved to be another behavior red zone. Vertically oriented Asia required daily elevator rides. Fortunately, Asians were remarkably tolerant, given the indignities my son inflicted on them, especially the people he met in elevators. An attractive neighbor wearing a breezy floral skirt only uttered a high-pitched, surprised squeal when Kendall reached out and touched her skirt in a strategically frontal location. At a resort in the Philippines, a rotund man in a hotel robe simply tousled Kendall's hair and remarked, "Good boy," after Kendall bounced his head on the man's ample belly.

Although embarrassing, those incidents were relatively harmless and not nearly as jarring as a total meltdown. Even so, with a child flailing and writhing on the floor of an elevator for a forty-story descent, my fellow passengers in Hong Kong politely ignored Kendall and me. I wanted to reward their tolerance with an explanation, but thirty seconds was never long enough to explain. Even when he licked the buttons before exiting the lift, I simply grimaced and hurried him along as best I could.

In space-challenged Hong Kong, parks were dual-purpose facilities serving two distinct demographics, children and the elderly. Each group had areas of the park designed for them. There were slides and monkey bars for children and exercise stations and benches for the elderly. Domestic helpers typically attended both groups. The whole point of public parks was to establish stress-free zones where children could safely run wild, unfettered by rules or restraint. How could a child get in trouble in a park?

Playing at a park near my son's school one afternoon, my son morphed into a force of anarchy and discord. His reign was brief but intense. The first victim of Kendall's curiosity was an elderly man exercising his arms. The man had set his cane to the side of the exercise station. Kendall was casually wandering past when the sight of the cane piqued his curiosity. Property rights, like religion, were a foreign concept to him. Walking just a few steps behind Kendall, I watched him snatch the man's cane off the ground. Kendall examined it as the bemused man looked on. I arrived and explained to Kendall that the cane was not ours and needed to be returned. Fortunately on this day Kendall relinquished the cane without a fight. The man was gracious and nodded and chuckled as I returned the cane to the ground next to the exercise station.

While I was doing this, something else caught Kendall's attention, and he was off. No sooner had I finished apologizing for this discourtesy than I looked up to see Kendall grab the handles of a wheelchair and push it along the park path. It was an occupied wheelchair. The occupant was an alarmed elderly woman. Kendall did not get far with the wheelchair because the elderly woman's caretaker and I reached the chair at about the same time. I persuaded Kendall to let go. He did, but now he showed signs of frustration. In the span of a few minutes, his modest desires were thwarted. He scrambled back to the children's play area only to latch on to a stroller parked there. Luckily it was empty, but by now I was a wreck. I had enough of the park, and the other park visitors probably had enough of us. We departed before we were forcibly ejected.

Not far from our apartment was a decent Italian restaurant. We often walked there for Sunday evening dinner. The front of the restaurant had glass French doors that opened to a spacious sidewalk. Adjacent to the sidewalk was a small car park. The children usually finished their pizza and pasta before Mark and I finished our main courses and asked if they could play in front. Since we could easily maintain visual contact with them, we agreed; after all, it was just a sidewalk; what could go wrong?

The first time we allowed the children to play in front while we finished our meal we discovered that the little devils had erased the chalkboard listing the restaurant specials. The following week we took pains to secure assurances from them that the chalkboard was off-limits. Once again, the area looked benign, so my son was allowed to wait outside while my husband paid the check. The restaurant employed a musician who wanted to sing a few duets with Brigitte. While I enjoyed their rendition of "When You Wish Upon a Star," I turned to check on Kendall. Words could barely form in my mouth.

"Mark...the...car."

Mark followed my gaze to where Kendall was perched on the roof of a sleek, black Ferrari. Mark moved with astonishing speed and flew out the door. He snatched Kendall off the roof of the car. Kendall began protesting immediately. Surely had Kendall been discovered by the vehicle's owner, we would have learned that even in Asia there were limits to tolerance.

THIRTY

....

THE DISTANCE BETWEEN HEAVEN AND HERE

I was dead and did not see a bright light and thought that was a bad sign. I seemed to be standing in a dark void. I wondered what I was supposed to do—wait or start walking? With no visual orientation, I had no idea which direction to set off in. Then I saw an old jalopy materialize and head towards me at high speed. The vehicle was of indeterminate make and model and inadvertently a convertible, with no windows and twisted stakes of metal all that remained of the former doorposts. I could make out two passengers as the vehicle approached, a rangy-looking driver with shards of white hair flapping maniacally around his face and a mousy woman, pale and small, seated in the back. The vehicle continued to accelerate, and I was beginning to think it was not going to stop for me. As the car drew closer, the driver slammed on the brakes, and I could make out his frenzied expression and his passenger's frightened one. Then I saw the cause for their concern, a pack of monstrous hounds was bearing down on them. The hounds' presence registered with me immediately; what did not was that they were there for me. The driver shouted at me, "Get in."

The vehicle never actually stopped, just slowed down, and I flung myself into the back seat, colliding with the other passenger. I sat upright and faced the woman, who was unfazed by my abrupt arrival, and instead remained transfixed on the hounds, because they were there for her too. The driver gunned it, but the hounds had gained. Ears flat against their heads, yellow eyes intent, lips raised in snarls bearing their impossibly long fangs while froth trailed down the fur of their thick necks. Not a single hound faltered or slowed. In fact, they were gaining on us. With an additional passenger, however, the jalopy was not moving as fast as before. We were not going to make it. Once again the driver addressed me, "Throw her out."

There is an old Irish saying, "May you be in heaven an hour before the devil knows you're dead." Were the Irish onto something regarding the transition between this life and the afterlife? This incident suggested that the afterlife was equivocal. Fingers crossed, I was hoping for Purgatory. Maybe the real battle began after the heart stopped beating? Perhaps a better person would have received a faster vehicle. Or maybe the hounds would not have been unleashed to retrieve their soul, allowing them an unconcerned stroll from this life to heaven's doorstep. This driver and vehicle, long past their prime, were the best a damaged soul like mine could hope for. My earthly demise had not escaped notice, and both sides were laying claim to my soul, albeit one less enthusiastically than the other. The point seemed to be, you get to heaven only if you can get to heaven. What was also clear, whatever my crimes, the other passenger's were worse. Still, it seemed wrong to sacrifice her to save myself, but I did it anyway.

Usually my dreams were odd bits and random images, but this one, possessing a narrative arc, seemed like a message. Was my dream of the afterlife a warning to mend my soul? I would be the first to admit, though perhaps not the only, that it was in bad need of repair.

I assumed moving to Hong Kong would fix everything. Kendall would get therapy that would cure him, Mark would join the family in a few months, and Brigitte would get the attention she deserved. Almost a year after our arrival and none of those things had come to pass.

When I arrived in Hong Kong with Kendall and Brigitte, Mark called every evening to check on us, and every night I cried into the phone. I was depressed. Depressed because I did not know how to do what I was supposed to be doing. The only thing worse than being bad at something was being bad at something you could not quit. I hated myself for not being able to buck up and get myself together. I wistfully recalled the days when my greatest troubles were unfriendly expat neighbors and crazy Chinese drivers.

I was not just perpetually weepy. After moving to Hong Kong with the children, I contemplated suicide, often. With more than 7,500 high-rise buildings, more than any other city in the world, Hong Kong was particularly conducive to suicide by jumping. There were many nights that I stood on the balcony of our apartment and looked down at the concrete walkway below, not out at the reflected lights shimmering on the black water. I was not there to admire the view. I was there to jump. Before the urge became an attempt, I retreated back into my apartment. What kept me from jumping? My children. I could not know with specificity what the consequences my suicide would hold for my children, but I knew it would be disastrous. Over time the impulse to end my own life eased. However, once the door was opened, it never fully closed again. Developing a sense of humor, or lightening up, is usually not viewed as a life or death matter for most people, but it was for me. My ability to attract luck included equal portions of good and bad. I was going to die an early death, either at my own hands or from rotting from the inside out, if I did not develop the ability to laugh about whatever came my way.

In April 2010 Mark's father died from a self-inflicted gunshot wound to the head. He had been in poor health and constant pain for a decade. His decision to end his own life, and therefore end his pain and misery, shocked and saddened the entire family in a way that succumbing to illness or old age would not. In addition to the persistent stigma of suicide, perhaps the survivors pondered their own culpability. Were they haunted by unanswerable questions: "Did they suspect anything was wrong?" or, "Was there more they could have done?" I did not want my actions to haunt anyone, ever.

Several months later, as Mark and I finished the steaks he grilled on our apartment balcony, the children tried on the Halloween costumes we purchased for them. Brigitte was a friendly witch, and Kendall was an astronaut. I looked up from where I sat at the table. I saw Kendall perched on a chair on the balcony, his little hand gripping the railing as he prepared to go over the side. Our apartment was on the forty-third floor.

"Mark, look at Kendall!"

Mark leapt up and quickly crossed the room to the balcony.

"Kendall, get down from that chair," he said in an insanely calm way.

Kendall stepped down reluctantly.

"But I want to fly like an astronaut and visit Papa in heaven," Kendall protested.

"Kendall, you only go to heaven once, at the very end of your life. That's a long time from now. Heaven isn't a place you get to visit," I said, finally finding my voice, despite my heart in my throat.

"Sorry, little man, we only get to fly on airplanes. We don't have wings like birds do," Mark added.

Good lord, I thought, *No wonder having children accelerates the aging process.* A prolonged diet of red meat might be bad for the arteries, but my children could stop my heart in an instant. Of all the things people told me that would change once I had children, one thing they neglected to mention was the near constant state of fear that would always be present, simmering below the surface. Fear that a moment's inattention, a chance encounter with evil or simply the capriciousness of life would rip from me the soul it was my responsibility to nurture and protect until adulthood. That responsibility is what kept me going. Finding my sense of humor made it bearable.

THIRTY-ONE

ROCKY MOUNTAIN REDEYE

Technically my passengers were not hitchhikers since I met them at the airport and not along an interstate. They probably told me their names, but remembering them was not my priority. Staying alive was my priority. The two anonymous dudes had joined Brigitte and me for the drive from Denver International Airport to the Vail Valley. I had made the drive before, during daylight, favorable weather conditions, and with people I actually knew. However, I had not braved it during the aggressive darkness of a winter storm. As if a snowstorm was not enough peril, I was operating on virtually no sleep after traveling for more than twenty hours from Hong Kong. The not-quite-hitchhikers did virtually nothing to aid in the journey, but I could not have done it without them. Their presence in my car and their untroubled attitude, real or not, gave me the confidence I needed to keep going when I wanted to pull over at the first Marriott I saw. If they could be composed, then I could resist the urge to give in to panic.

Jet lag kicked my ass. My strategy was to gut it out and refrain from napping, but I still woke up in the wee hours of the morning only to remain semi-comatose and bleary-eyed for the remainder of the day. That went on for days. Brigitte was not much better. For the Christmas break in 2010, I decided to depart with Brigitte from Hong Kong a week earlier than Mark and Kendall, in the hope that we would be over jet lag by the time the guys arrived. Mark and Kendall bounce back from massive time changes with astonishing ease. Also, Kendall's school was parsimonious with breaks and only gave him a week off at Christmas. He took another week, which they allowed grudgingly. With Brigitte still in preschool, her schedule was slightly more flexible, so we took three weeks. By the time Mark and Kendall showed up, I hoped that Brigitte and I would be fully recovered and functional.

Our travel day began ominously. After we boarded the plane and had stowed our belongings, Brigitte began examining the headphones left on her seat. As the slow rumba-line of passengers shuffled past our row, a family with a daughter about Brigitte's age came to a stop next to our seats.

The girl held up her doll to Brigitte and said, "This is my baby."

In response, Brigitte held up the plug-in end of her headphones and said, "This is my gun."

State-Sponsored Sex

Thankfully the line started moving before Brigitte made any more statements that might prompt the intervention of an air marshal.

Air travel across the Pacific was a long slog. Hong Kong to San Francisco was typically fourteen hours of recycled air and economy seat torment. Customs and Immigration at the San Francisco airport were usually efficient, but the system started to break down with the security reentry. U.S. airports were not designed for the stringent security of a post-9/11 world. In San Francisco, the security areas were small, with slow-moving, serpentine lines. Still, once we arrived at this point, we started to breathe easier, as we were more than halfway home.

Once we touched down in Denver, it was just one more connection, and we could claim our bags, hop in our car parked at the Eagle County airport and walk through our front door thirty minutes later. Running into a friend at Denver's airport reinforced the feeling that we were back home. That feeling came to an abrupt halt when we arrived at the gate for our short flight to Eagle County. Instead of a gate agent, a pilot addressed the assembled crowd of passengers. Not a good sign.

"Sorry, folks. Due to bad weather, our flight to Eagle County has been cancelled. Please see customer service to reschedule your flights."

Brigitte and I joined the crowd of weather refugees trudging off to the closest customer service counter. A long line greeted our arrival. The only movement seemed to be people shifting their weight from their right to their left leg. Two guys at the front of the line turned around, and one of them addressed the crowd.

"We're heading to Vail. Anyone interested in sharing a rental car?"

My hand shot up like a kindergartener's. "We're in."

The two guys collected the bags while Brigitte and I headed off to the rental car facility to rent whatever seemed as if it might make it over Vail Pass in a blizzard. We returned with a Ford Explorer. I drove, one guy sat in the passenger seat and the other sat in back with Brigitte. Brigitte immediately fell asleep. We set out for the mountains, not sure what to expect. It was snowing hard. I stayed in second gear most of the way, and the speedometer never registered more than forty miles per hour. My passengers were two guys from Ohio. I do not recall anything about them despite the fact that we chatted the entire drive. A drive that normally took two hours, that night stretched to nearly four. They were likely used to snowy weather. Having lived in Shanghai and Hong Kong for the better part of a decade, I was not. I was also not used to driving on the right, but I did not tell them that. I just kept motoring.

The distance from DIA to Vail was more than a hundred miles and involves navigating two major mountain passes, the Eisenhower Pass at more than 11,000 feet above sea level and Vail Pass at 10,662 feet. Transiting both passes was I-70, a four-lane, divided highway. A few small towns dot the route from Denver

State-Sponsored Sex

to Vail, but most of the land was national forest or wilderness. After sunset, headlights struggle against the pervasive darkness of the wilderness in the best of conditions. The thick, relentless flurries falling that night reduced visibility to no more than a few car lengths. Emerging from the Eisenhower tunnel and beginning the steady descent towards Dillon and Frisco, I had the sensation that I was driving off the edge of the world. My fingernails dug deeper into the foam steering wheel covering, and I pressed my left foot harder to the floor. I screwed up the courage to remain calm and continued driving.

There were a few other dicey moments. The scariest incident occurred when Brigitte woke up just west of Vail Pass and noticed an unfamiliar face staring back at her. She started to scream. Backseat guy agreed to take over driving, but we needed to get to the right-hand side of the highway. As I attempted to maneuver the car to the right shoulder, another driver decided to pass our vehicle, on the right. Somehow we did not collide.

Fortunately the Vail exit was only a few more miles. As we emerged into the cozy valley beneath the Gore Range, the snow stopped and the moon shone brightly through breaks in the clouds. Brigitte calmed down, and we soon arrived at our passenger's condo. We laughed a little about the harrowing drive, wished one another a happy holiday and said our goodbyes.

As I drove away, I realized that if Mark had been there, I would have allowed him to do the driving. I would have not thought myself capable of navigating that route in a winter storm. I wondered, if I could do that, what else could I do?

As an air force cadet in college, I attended Recondo Training at Ft. Riley Army Base in Kansas. When the other cadets and I arrived at the rappelling tower and sat down in the bleachers, I thought, *How nice, a rappelling demonstration.* When I was handed a helmet and gloves, I realized it was no demonstration. I also thought, *No way.* Once I learned how to do it, however, they could not get me off the tower. How many things have I convinced myself I could not do before I even tried? The thought was staggering. But there I was, years later, relearning that lesson.

Somewhere in the intervening years I had accepted that I could not do things. I relinquished running my life. Mr. Chang did the driving. First Xiao Yin, and later Coly, did the cleaning. Xiao Yin would not even let me carry the groceries into the house. I let Mark do the challenging things; he managed the finances and ordered the wine. I accepted my role as the secondary partner in our marriage, forgetting how much I had done on my own. I had done all the paperwork and coordination to adopt Brigitte. I had been Kendall's advocate and researcher. I had taken on the full-time parenting so Mark could keep his job and Kendall could get the best care possible. I was my own worse critic, not counting my sister. I may have never made the cheerleading squad in high school, but it was not too

State-Sponsored Sex

late to start cheering for myself now. Nobody else seemed to be lining up.

THIRTY-TWO

THE BITCH IN THE KITCHEN

One of the worst things about being a housewife is the censorship from other members of the profession.

"You don't swear in front of your children?" another mother asked as we waited for our children outside the Hong Kong preschool Brigitte attended. My vigilance must have momentarily lapsed, and I inadvertently exposed myself as the potty-mouthed mother I was. I responded with a strained smile, hopefully disguising my true impulse, which was to go all Samuel L. Jackson on her ass, *Bitch, those little fuckers are the reason I cuss.*

I do not recall foul language comprising a large amount of my vocabulary in the past, probably because I had nothing to curse about. Moving to Hong Kong and confronting the increased burden of caring for two children who were attending different schools and further complicated by Kendall's special diet and therapy sessions were fertile ground for profane language. But maybe it was just the two children part.

"Mom, are you a veter...veteranaran?" Brigitte asked.

"You mean a veterinarian? A doctor who takes care of animals?"
"Yeah."
"Not yeah."
"I mean, yes, Mom."
"No, I'm not. I'm a housewife."
"You mean you're nothing, just a housewife?"
"Just a housewife."

This conversation got me thinking that seen and not heard needed to make a comeback. Of all the anachronistic social customs jettisoned in the last century, why did we do away with the universal gag order on children? Of course, Brigitte had a point. With few barriers to entry and no formal training required, anyone could be a housewife. But why would they want to? The pay was bad, the hours were long, forget about days off or ever getting sick. Worse still, it was a customer service nightmare.

I could have been a mash-up of Rachel Ray, Jaime Oliver and Martha Stewart and I would still be subjected to, "I'm not eating that. It looks yucky."

"But you haven't even tried it."

"I'm not eating that. It's green, *and* it looks yucky."

Every day I dared them to fire me. After a while, it looked like they were actually considering the offer.

Back in Shanghai I was a housewife in name only. I had none of the duties usually associated with housekeeping such as childrearing, cooking or cleaning. The only constant was that I also had no income. Being

State-Sponsored Sex

a housewife was never one of my life plans, and I have had many and varied plans. Like unions and smokers, it was membership in a dying breed. Housewives were like an endangered species that no one wanted to save.

Is anyone ever really prepared for all of life's possibilities? I was not, and because I did not expect anything to change, I made no attempts to upgrade my domestic skill set. After Shanghai, I became the sausage-making equivalent to a housewife—not a pretty sight but the job got done, cursing was just part of the package. I traded spa appointments and lunch with the ladies for play dates and room parent duty. Unlike the characters in the made-for-TV movie, *The Stepford Wives*, I was not offed and replaced by a fembot. I domesticated myself. I resumed the duty I did for allowance money in high school—house cleaning. At ten dollars a week for my services, I made more in 1984 than I did in 2010. Worse still, there had been tremendous scope-creep in the intervening years. Now my job expanded to include cooking, laundering, childcare and chauffeuring.

High school home economics would have provided a useful skill set, if my father had allowed me to take it. Once parenthood entered the equation, cooking classes became more of a necessity than a social diversion and long lunches became history. Hong Kong's YMCA offered an impressive array of adult education classes, but being an efficient housewife was not one of them. My other go-to resource was Google. I typed the word "housewife" into the search function, and one interesting search it returned was "Online Valium, No Prescription." More than forty years ago the Rolling Stones sang about barbiturate use amongst housewives in their hit song "Mother's Little Helper." Trolling the Internet for drugs indicated that the perceived need for medically enhanced relaxation still existed; only the method of acquisition was upgraded.

But why would a housewife need to medicate? I mean, how hard could housekeeping be? That would have been my line of reasoning during my pre-family days, back when achievements were both measurable and monetarily rewarded, when conversations were held with other college-educated adults and well before I was intimately involved in my children's digestive process, from start to finish, before my transformation into a housewife, in name and deed. As someone who rarely remembered to stock aspirin, my other thought was, *Why didn't I think of drugs sooner?*

With no imminent remedy to my domestic shortcomings, another option emerged that required minimal effort on my part, divine intervention. I needed a patron saint. As soon as this idea occurred to me, I dismissed it as absurd. *Seriously, a patron saint of housewives?* Then I Googled "patron saints" and discovered they number in the thousands. If sore throats, St. Blaise; cattle, St. Cornelius; and archers, St. Sebastian, were worthy of patron saints, surely the most important job in the world has one.

State-Sponsored Sex

Actually, housewives have four, the same as brewers, and they were all lame. They were primarily saints by relation, a massive case of ecclesiastical nepotism. This from an organization no stranger to scandal. St. Anne was Mary's mother, her one claim to fame and about all we know about her. St. Martha? Sister of St. Lazarus. St. Monica was the mother of St. Augustine. St. Zita, which, by the way, does not even sound like a Catholic name, was a servant who gave away the household's food. I do not call that a saint, I call that unemployed. None of these broads inspired confidence. Each one was defined by whom she was related to, rather than what she accomplished. Come to think of it, that sounded a lot like me. Ten thousand saints and not one was a housewife who led troops in a battle, fought off wild animals or defied a pharaoh? And frankly, as far as I could tell, none were responsible for any miracles. I considered it a miracle my children had all their digits, mostly, and their eyesight, and no one was fast-tracking me for beatification.

THIRTY-THREE

RILEY'S WIFE

"I want your life," the Citibank customer service representative said to me, in a voice raised in New York but aged in tobacco. She then assured me that I had indeed reached a call center in Tampa, Florida, not Pune, India, that evening after I had endured innumerable computer-generated messages before finally connecting with a real, live human being. The representative blurted this out during the course of our conversation that was being recorded for quality and training purposes. Despite my longevity as a Citibank cardholder, at more than fifteen years it was one of my only long-term relationships, they frequently turned off my access to credit for my protection, but mostly theirs.

These conversations were maddeningly similar. "But I live overseas," I explained once again, "and have for more than a decade." Somehow this information never got posted to my account, and eventually the well of credit would once again run dry.

Admittedly, with credit card charges made in Bangkok, Hong Kong and Macau all in the previous six weeks, my life looked rather exciting on paper if the realities of economy-class air travel accompanied by small children were not considered. This representative saw my charges and made assumptions that bore only a passing resemblance to reality. There would have been a time when I would have smugly agreed with her; I did have it pretty easy, for a while. Explaining my journey from successful but solitary singleton to adventurous expat to harried housewife, my own downward mobility spiral, would take longer than the average customer service phone call.

In June of 2000, after my arrival in Hong Kong, I sent my brother Robert an email in which I claimed to be living the life of Riley. He responded, "Who is Riley, anyway? And does he know you have his life?" The precise origins of the phrase were debatable, but the Irish-American community popularized the expression in the early twentieth century. It was hard to know what specifically constituted the good life to the Irish-American working class, but married to a successful executive, living in a posh Hong Kong hotel suite and traveling throughout Asia and Europe seemed close enough. If its exact parameters were undefined, Riley's life was acknowledged as exclusive, and likely ephemeral, something to be momentarily enjoyed while it lasted. When I sent my brother that email, I thought I had Riley's life and had no intention of relinquishing it, as if

State-Sponsored Sex

I had a choice in the matter. At that moment my life was going better than I could have imagined and not remotely how I had planned.

More than a decade later, and with two kids in tow, I was no longer living the life of Riley. I was more like the wife of Riley. Housewife was my only remaining ongoing endeavor despite my efforts to undermine even it. As for my other projects, Chinese cultural immersion fizzled after just a few months. Learning Mandarin staggered along a little bit longer. The nail salon was over before it even started due to my unanticipated aversion to other people's feet. I heard the farmers' market kept going until the developer closed the neighborhood.

A new undertaking beckoned a few years after moving to Hong Kong. The City University of Hong Kong advertised a Master of Fine Arts in Creative Nonfiction Writing on the front page of the *South China Morning Post* in the spring of 2010. By chance, I saw the advertisement on a Sunday morning as I casually glanced at the paper. My first thought was, *You can get a degree in that?* My second was, *I'm going to apply.* I had no intention of telling anyone my plan, or actually attending the program. I had participated in two writing classes to that point—an online Gotham Writer's Workshop that was encouraging and a Hong Kong YMCA class that was not. If I was accepted by the City U program, I would take that as a sign that my Gotham classmates were correct and my writing was decent. If rejected, I would know that those bitches at the Y were right, I did suck. Stealth mode would spare me public embarrassment.

However, the graduate school application process involved ordering transcripts, writing essays and finding several credible-sounding people to write letters of recommendation. Transcripts and essays were not difficult to conceal, but letters of recommendation were. I asked the only two PhDs I knew in Hong Kong to write letters for me. Fearing inevitable detection, I came clean with Mark. He surprised me. He was sure that I would be accepted and insistent that I attend when I was.

Preparing my application forced me to decide, and explain, what kind of writer I was, what did I bring to this program and what did I hope to get out of it. I doubted the world needed another melancholy Irish-American writer. My Gotham classmates had found some of my writing humorous. Never mind what my YMCA classmates found, they had been discredited. Preparing my City U application, I experienced an epiphany about the kind of writing I wanted to attempt. I was going to write humor. Up until then, I never thought of myself as a funny person, but it was not my fault. I was doomed from the beginning. My parents named me Deirdre, from the Irish myth "Deirdre of the Sorrows." It was not so much a name as a curse. Through writing, I discovered I could break that curse. My intention was to employ humor, not to trivialize the events of my life, but to bear them. I belatedly realized

State-Sponsored Sex

that a little humor would have gone a long way in confronting the challenges of the years since Kendall's autism diagnosis. Heck, a sense of humor would have made my entire life up to that point easier. Changing my writing perspective changed my life perspective. Also, after forty years I realized I could just start going by my middle name.

THIRTY-FOUR

DANCING WITH ERICA JONG

I was out of gummi bears and trying not to think about the possible ramifications. Instead, I concentrated on the excitement I felt because I was seated next to Erica Jong, *the* Erica Jong, author of the bestseller and sexual revolution manifesto *Fear of Flying*. As Erica addressed the group of writers gathered from around the world to attend her writing workshop for the coming week, my eyes were reluctantly drawn to movement behind her head. A glass wall separated our conference room from the lobby. On the other side of that transparent wall, my son, Kendall, was demonstrating dance moves he learned from Wii Dance. As he admired his reflected gyrations in the glass, Kendall was oblivious to the roomful of women on the other side of the glass now watching him.

I was two semesters into my MFA at City U in Hong Kong and immersing myself in the world of writing by attending workshops, reading literary magazines, submitting essays to literary magazines and getting rejected by literary magazines. Success, I assured myself, would be so much sweeter after an initiation period of rejection. I just hoped my initiation period did not outlive me. My presence in Erica's workshop was a small but thrilling success. It was a juried memoir workshop at the Aspen Literary Festival that required submitting a sample of my writing. I did not win an award or have my writing published, but based on my writing sample, I was one of twelve women selected to attend Erica's weeklong workshop.

Erica's much-anticipated arrival was an hour later than scheduled. An hour earlier I stashed Brigitte and Kendall outside on a spacious terrace surrounded by woods at the idyllically located Aspen Institute, where our class was being held during the Festival. Equipped with as diverse a selection of children's paraphernalia as I could cram into their backpacks, I figured Kendall and Brigitte had enough to keep them occupied for at least a little while. What I did not anticipate was the hour wait for our delayed instructor. Even in late June, Aspen can be chilly. As afternoon transitioned to evening, the air was definitely developing a crisp bite. I had hoped to keep them out of sight until the orientation was over and my lack of appropriate childcare went undetected. But cold kids can quickly become cranky, complaining kids, so I moved them into a small nook at the top of the stairs, just outside the lobby separating the conference room containing the memoir writers, where I was, with the room across the lobby containing the fiction writers.

State-Sponsored Sex

Kendall and Brigitte had been unusually well behaved for the last hour, but they'd reached their limit. I made the quick mental calculation that I was unlikely to succeed in persuading Kendall to return to a quiet, unobtrusive activity like reading or spelling with his Bananagrams. Also, and more critically, there was the gummi bear deficit to consider. Those rubbery blobs were the ultimate bribery tool in my parenting arsenal; without them I had no leverage.

The best I could do in this situation was retreat. Attempts to quiet my children, Kendall in particular, would likely prove distracting to my classmates. After all, it was just an orientation. I thought I was only required to register that afternoon. I did not even know I was expected to attend an orientation until I reread the program more thoroughly over breakfast, hence the lack of organized childcare. The important part was the generative workshop that began the following morning. At that time, the kids would be securely occupied with summer camp, and I would continue the effort to channel my creativity into something other than disguising the vegetable content of dinner or removing dried bodily secretions from household surfaces without also removing paint or finish.

Erica, who had no idea a *Dancing with the Stars* moment was occurring behind her head, stopped speaking and shot me a questioning glance as I gathered my belongings and mumbled an apology. I doubt many people get up and walk out on Erica Jong. However, she was a mom, as were most of the women in the class. I suspected that I was not the first or the only woman in the room to have some long-anticipated event curtailed or missed entirely because of the necessity to respond to the needs of my children.

Acceptance. That was the mantra I repeated to myself as I herded the children towards the parking lot. I got the idea from an old Tom Selleck comedy from the early 1990s, *Mr. Baseball*, in which he played an aging major league baseball player traded to a Japanese team. He arrived in Japan with a disparaging attitude towards everything Japanese. In time, he realized that he could not change Japanese culture. Eventually, he began to practice acceptance and repeated the word as a reminder. I learned that I could not choose when I parented. I continued to repeat the word "acceptance," but unlike Selleck's character Jack Elliot, I lacked a sensei to guide me. My only rational options were to accept and adjust. Oh, I could fume for the rest of the evening. God knows I had done a lot of that over the years and would likely continue doing so for the foreseeable future. But that night I was reconciled to the fact that my children had tried to behave. Unlike other times when I am convinced they were punishment for severe transgressions on my part in a past life.

In addition to a more Zen-like approach to parenting, I came to realize that my concept of adventure, largely unchanged since childhood, had been immaturely defined. My exaggerated role models for adventure

State-Sponsored Sex

included James Bond and Indiana Jones. While focusing on global intrigue and international travel, I failed to focus on the adventures, and misadventures, of everyday life. More importantly, I realized that the difference between the two was determined by my sense of humor.

The ability to laugh at life and myself was not a trivial matter. It was not hyperbole to say that developing a sense of humor was a matter of life and death for me. I was a very late bloomer developing my ability to laugh at myself. Desperation convinced me to laugh like my life depended on it, because it did. It was comforting to know that I was not alone. In 1928 Mahatma Gandhi wrote, "If I had no sense of humor, I would long ago have committed suicide." That made two of us.

Kendall's "dance-capade," while mortifying at the time, became one of my favorite memories from my memorable week in Aspen, which seemed appropriate because Erica's book, *Fear of Flying*, was really about fearlessness. I did not understand that when I read it at sixteen while living in Heidelberg. I thought it was about sex. Even though wise adults had attempted over the years to communicate the importance of letting go of my fears, it was raising children that finally made the lesson stick. Paradoxically, I do fear, every day, about important things like their safety and security. However, I have let go of fear of the trivial, mostly. Watching my children dance and play like no one was watching convinced me that most of the time, no one was watching, and even when they were, it did not matter anyway. Some people can be told that, and get it. However, people like me need to discover it for themselves.

Acknowledgements

Thank you for reading my book. If you enjoyed it, won't you please take a moment to leave me a review?

I also want to thank my family, especially Mark, Kendall and Brigitte, for their love and support as well as providing a steady stream of writing material, whether they meant to or not. Thanks are also extended to Xu Xi, the Writer-in-Residence at the English Department of the City University of Hong Kong, who oversees the MFA program, as well as the outstanding international faculty and student body that make the City U program the best writing incubator an aspiring author could hope to experience. Thanks to Jane Dixon-Smith for the cover design and Joanna Penn at thecreativepenn.com for her encouragement and support of independent authors.

ABOUT THE AUTHOR

Claire Noble is a May 2012 graduate of the inaugural cohort of the City University of Hong Kong Master of Fine Arts in Creative Writing Program. She lives with her family in Switzerland where she is a chronic room parent and occasional stand-up comic. Find Claire online at www.clairenoble.org and on Twitter @thehkhousewife

Made in the USA
Charleston, SC
23 June 2014